123 Creative Cheesecake Recipes

(123 Creative Cheesecake Recipes - Volume 1)

Victoria Klein

Content

123 AWESOME CHEESECAKE RECIPES . 5

1. 3 Step PHILADELPHIA Mini Cheesecakes 5
2. Almond Macaroon Cheesecake 5
3. Ancho Chocolate Cheesecake 6
4. Apple Pie Cheesecakes 6
5. Apple Pecan Cheesecake 7
6. Berry Bliss No Bake Cheesecake 7
7. Bird's Nest Mini Baked Cheesecakes 8
8. Bit Of Irish Cheesecake 8
9. Bite Size Salted Caramel Cheesecakes 9
10. Black Forest Cheesecake 10
11. Blossoming Berry Cheesecake 10
12. Blueberry Cheesecake Bars 11
13. Butter Pecan Cheesecake 11
14. Cappuccino Cheesecake 12
15. Caramel Bourbon Cheesecake Bites 13
16. Caramel Pumpkin Mousse Tart 13
17. Centennial Cheesecake 14
18. Cheesecake Fruit Dip 15
19. Cheesecake Topper 15
20. Cherry Cheesecake 16
21. Cherry Cheesecake Recipe 16
22. Chocolate Cheesecake Flan 17
23. Chocolate Cheesecake Ice Cream Cake 17
24. Chocolate Mint Cookie Cheesecake 18
25. Chocolate Truffle Cheesecake 18
26. Chocolate Velvet Cheesecake 19
27. Chocolate Orange Cheesecake 20
28. Chocolate Orange Cheesecake Layer Cake 20
29. Cinnamon Streusel Pumpkin Cheesecake Bars 21
30. Citrus Gelatin Layered Cheesecake 22
31. Coconut Lime Cheesecake 22
32. Coconut Strawberry Banana Bars 23
33. Coffee Cheesecake Pie 24
34. Creamy No Bake Chocolate Pudding Cheesecake 24
35. Cupid's Cherry Cheesecakes 25
36. Double Lemon Cheesecake 25
37. Double Decker OREO Cheesecake 26
38. Dulce De Leche Swirl Cheesecake 26
39. Easy Caramel Pecan Cheesecake 27
40. Easy Mini Cheesecakes 27
41. Eggnog Cheesecake Recipe 28
42. English Toffee Cheesecake 28
43. Festive Irish Cream Cheesecake 29
44. Frozen Lemon Blueberry Cheesecake 30
45. Frozen Mini Cinnamon Coffee Cheesecakes 30
46. JELL O® Eggnog Cheesecake 31
47. JELL O® No Bake Pineapple Cheesecake Bars 31
48. Key Lime Mini Cheesecakes 32
49. Layered Coconut Cream Cheesecake Bars 32
50. Lemon Meringue Cheesecake 33
51. Lemon Refrigerator Cheesecake 34
52. Lemon Blueberry Cheesecake Jars 34
53. Lemon White Chocolate Mini Cheesecakes 35
54. Low Fat Orange Dream Cheesecake 35
55. Marbled Chocolate Cheesecake 36
56. Marshmallow Cookie Cheesecake 36
57. Mini Classic Cheesecake Recipe 37
58. Mini Coconut Cheesecakes Bites 37
59. Mini Lemon Cheesecakes 38
60. Mini Pumpkin Spice Latte Cheesecakes 39
61. Mini Strawberry Cheesecakes 39
62. Mocha Cheesecake Minis 40
63. New York Style Mini Cheesecake Bites 40
64. No Bake Cheesecake Bars 41
65. No Bake OREO Cheesecake Recipe 41
66. No Bake Orange Cheesecake 42
67. No Bake Strawberry Banana Smoothie Cheesecake 42
68. OREO Peanut Butter Cheesecake 43
69. OREO Pumpkin Cheesecake 43
70. Our Best Chocolate Cheesecake 44
71. PHILADELPHIA "Fruit Smoothie" No Bake Cheesecake 44
72. PHILADELPHIA 3 STEP Chocolate Chip Cookie Dough Cheesecake 45
73. PHILADELPHIA 3 STEP OREO Cheesecake 45
74. PHILADELPHIA 3 STEP Peppermint Cheesecake 46
75. PHILADELPHIA 3 STEP Pumpkin Cheesecake 46
76. PHILADELPHIA 3 Step Chocolate Chip

Cheesecake...47

77.   PHILADELPHIA Black Forest Cheesecake 47

78.   PHILADELPHIA Caramel Nut Cheesecake...48

79.   PHILADELPHIA Classic Cheesecake 48

80.   PHILADELPHIA Easter Mini Cheesecakes 49

81.   PHILADELPHIA New York Cheesecake Bars 49

82.   PHILADELPHIA New York Chocolate Cheesecake...50

83.   PHILADELPHIA New York Style Strawberry Swirl Cheesecake 51

84.   PHILADELPHIA No Bake Cheesecake..51

85.   PHILADELPHIA No Bake Peach Cheesecake...52

86.   PHILADELPHIA Peanut Butter Chocolate Cheesecake...52

87.   PHILADELPHIA OREO No Bake Cheesecake...53

88.   PHILADELPHIA® 3 STEP® Macaroon Cheesecake...53

89.   PHILADELPHIA® 3 STEP® Pina Colada Cheesecake...54

90.   PHILLY OREO Cheesecake Recipe.........54

91.   PLANTERS Almond Cheesecake 55

92.   Passion Fruit Cheesecake............................55

93.   Peanut Butter Mini Cheesecakes 56

94.   Peppermint Bark Cheesecake.....................57

95.   Pineapple No Bake Cheesecake Dessert...57

96.   Pineapple Upside Down Cheesecake 58

97.   Pumpkin Cheesecake 58

98.   Pumpkin Dump Cake With Pudding Topping..59

99.   Pumpkin Spiced Cheesecake......................59

100. Pumpkin Swirl Cheesecake.........................60

101. Quick Cheesecake 61

102. Quick Mini Pudding Cheesecakes.............61

103. Refrigerated Cranberry Cheesecake 61

104. Rice Pudding Cheesecake 62

105. Roasted Strawberry Pistachio Mini Cheesecakes...63

106. Smart Choice Creamy Pumpkin Pie..........63

107. Spiced Maple Walnut Cheesecake 64

108. Spiced Pumpkin Cheesecake Brownies.....64

109. Strawberry Cheesecake Ice Cream Cake ...65

110. Strawberry Cheesecake Smoothie..............66

111. Strawberry Cheesecake Squares 66

112. Strawberry Cheesecake With Sour Cream.66

113. Strawberry Rhubarb Cheesecake 67

114. Tiramisu Cheese Pie 68

115. Tiramisu Cheesecake....................................68

116. Tiramisu Mousse Cheesecake......................69

117. Toasted Almond Cheesecake Pie...............69

118. Triple Berry Cheesecake Tart 70

119. Two Tone Chocolate Cheesecake 71

120. Vanilla Cherry Cheesecake..........................71

121. Very Vanilla Custard Topped Cheesecake 72

122. White Chocolate Cheesecake 72

123. Zesty Lemon Cheesecake............................73

INDEX 74

CONCLUSION 76

123 Awesome Cheesecake Recipes

***

1. 3 Step PHILADELPHIA Mini Cheesecakes

Serving: 12 | Prep: 10mins | Cook: 4hours | Ready in: 4hours10mins

Ingredients

- 2 pkg. (8 oz. each) PHILADELPHIA Cream Cheese, softened
- 1/2 cup sugar
- 1/2 tsp. vanilla
- 2 eggs
- 12 OREO Cookies
- 1 kiwi
- 1/2 cup fresh blueberries
- 1/3 cup fresh raspberries

Direction

- Heat oven to 350°F.
- Beat cream cheese, sugar and vanilla with mixer until blended. Add eggs; mix just until blended.
- Place 1 cookie in each of 12 paper-lined muffin cups; top with cream cheese mixture.
- Bake 20 min. or until centers are almost set. Cool. Refrigerate 3 hours. Peel kiwi; cut into 6 slices, then cut each slice in half. Place 1 kiwi piece on each cheesecake. Top with berries.

Nutrition Information

- Calories: 230
- Protein: 4 g
- Cholesterol: 80 mg
- Sodium: 200 mg
- Total Carbohydrate: 0 g
- Sugar: 0 g
- Total Fat: 16 g
- Saturated Fat: 9 g
- Fiber: 1 g

2. Almond Macaroon Cheesecake

Serving: 16 | Prep: 30mins | Cook: 5hours | Ready in: 5hours30mins

Ingredients

- 1 pkg. (7 oz.) BAKER'S ANGEL FLAKE Coconut, lightly toasted
- 1/2 cup finely chopped, lightly toasted PLANTERS Slivered Almonds
- 1 can (14 oz.) sweetened condensed milk, divided
- 1/3 cup flour
- 1/4 cup (1/2 stick) butter or margarine, melted
- 4 pkg. (8 oz. each) PHILADELPHIA Cream Cheese, softened
- 1/4 cup sugar
- 4 egg s
- 1/4 cup almond-flavored liqueur

Direction

- Preheat oven to 325°F if using a greased silver 9-inch springform pan (or to 300°F if using a dark nonstick 9-inch springform pan). Mix coconut, almonds, 1/2 cup of the sweetened condensed milk, flour and butter until well blended; press onto bottom of pan.
- Beat cream cheese, sugar and remaining 3/4 cup sweetened condensed milk with electric mixer on medium speed until well blended. Add eggs, 1 at a time, mixing on low speed after each addition just until blended. Blend in liqueur; pour over crust.

- Bake 55 to 1 hour or until center is almost set. Run knife or metal spatula around rim of pan to loosen cake; cool before removing rim of pan. Refrigerate 4 hours or overnight. Store leftover cheesecake in refrigerator.

Nutrition Information

- Calories: 440
- Fiber: 2 g
- Total Fat: 32 g
- Cholesterol: 130 mg
- Total Carbohydrate: 28 g
- Protein: 8 g
- Sodium: 340 mg
- Sugar: 23 g
- Saturated Fat: 20 g

3. Ancho Chocolate Cheesecake

Serving: 16 | Prep: 20mins | Cook: 6hours10mins | Ready in: 6hours30mins

Ingredients

- 18 OREO Cookies, crushed (about 2 cups)
- 2 Tbsp. butter or margarine, melted
- 4 pkg. (8 oz. each) PHILADELPHIA Cream Cheese, softened
- 1 cup sugar
- 2 Tbsp. ancho chile pepper powder
- 1-1/2 pkg. (4 oz. each) BAKER'S Bittersweet Chocolate (6 oz.), broken into pieces, melted
- 4 egg s

Direction

- Heat oven to 325ºF.
- Mix crumbs and butter; press onto bottom of 9-inch springform pan.
- Beat cream cheese and sugar with mixer until blended. Add pepper powder and chocolate; mix well. Add eggs, 1 at a time, beating on low

speed after each just until blended; pour over crust.
- Bake 1 hour 10 min. or until center is almost set. Run knife around rim of pan to loosen cake; cool before removing rim. Refrigerate 4 hours.

Nutrition Information

- Calories: 380
- Protein: 6 g
- Fiber: 2 g
- Total Fat: 28 g
- Sugar: 23 g
- Saturated Fat: 16 g
- Cholesterol: 125 mg
- Total Carbohydrate: 30 g
- Sodium: 310 mg

4. Apple Pie Cheesecakes

Serving: 12 | Prep: 20mins | Cook: 3hours | Ready in: 3hours20mins

Ingredients

- 1 cup graham cracker crumbs
- 3/4 cup plus 3 Tbsp. sugar, divided
- 3 Tbsp. butter or margarine, melted
- 3 pkg. (8 oz. each) PHILADELPHIA Cream Cheese, softened
- 1 tsp. vanilla
- 1/2 tsp. ground cinnamon
- 3 eggs
- 1 can (21 oz.) apple pie filling

Direction

- Heat oven to 325°F.
- Combine graham crumbs, 3 Tbsp. sugar and butter; press onto bottoms of 12 paper-lined muffin cups.
- Beat cream cheese, vanilla, cinnamon and remaining sugar with mixer until blended.

- Add eggs, 1 at a time, mixing on low speed after each just until blended; spoon over crusts.
- Bake 25 to 30 min. or until centers of cheesecakes are almost set. Cool completely.
- Refrigerate 2 hours. Top with pie filling just before serving.

Nutrition Information

- Calories: 360
- Total Fat: 24 g
- Total Carbohydrate: 30 g
- Sodium: 260 mg
- Protein: 6 g
- Saturated Fat: 14 g
- Cholesterol: 110 mg
- Sugar: 24 g
- Fiber: 1 g

5. Apple Pecan Cheesecake

Serving: 16 | Prep: 15mins | Cook: 5hours55mins | Ready in: 6hours10mins

Ingredients

- 1-1/2 cups graham cracker crumbs
- 1/4 cup butter, melted
- 2 Tbsp. brown sugar
- 4 pkg. (8 oz. each) PHILADELPHIA Cream Cheese, softened
- 1-1/2 cups packed brown sugar, divided
- 1 tsp. vanilla
- 1 cup BREAKSTONE'S or KNUDSEN Sour Cream
- 4 eggs
- 3 Granny Smith apples, peeled, chopped
- 3/4 cup chopped PLANTERS Pecans
- 1 tsp. ground cinnamon

Direction

- Heat oven to 325°F.

- Line 13x9-inch pan with foil, with ends of foil extending over sides. Mix graham crumbs, butter and 2 Tbsp. sugar; press onto bottom of prepared pan.
- Beat cream cheese, 1 cup brown sugar and vanilla in large bowl with mixer until blended. Add sour cream; mix well. Add eggs, 1 at a time, mixing on low speed after each just until blended. Pour over crust. Combine apples, nuts, cinnamon and remaining sugar; spoon over cream cheese batter.
- Bake 55 min. or until center is almost set. Cool completely. Refrigerate 4 hours. Use foil handles to lift cheesecake from pan before cutting to serve.

Nutrition Information

- Calories: 430
- Total Fat: 30 g
- Total Carbohydrate: 35 g
- Sugar: 28 g
- Sodium: 320 mg
- Fiber: 1 g
- Saturated Fat: 16 g
- Cholesterol: 140 mg
- Protein: 7 g

6. Berry Bliss No Bake Cheesecake

Serving: 16 | Prep: 20mins | Cook: 6hours | Ready in: 6hours20mins

Ingredients

- 1 cup graham cracker crumbs
- 1/4 cup butter, melted
- 4 cups mixed fresh berries (blueberries, blackberries, raspberries, halved strawberries), divided
- 1 cup sugar, divided
- 3 pkg. (8 oz. each) PHILADELPHIA Cream Cheese, softened

- 2 cups thawed COOL WHIP Whipped Topping

Direction

- Mix graham crumbs and butter; press onto bottom of 9-inch springform pan.
- Mash 2 cups berries with 1/4 cup sugar in medium bowl. Beat cream cheese and remaining sugar in large bowl with mixer until blended. Add mashed berries; beat on low speed just until blended. Gently stir in COOL WHIP; spoon over crust.
- Refrigerate 6 hours. Run knife around rim of pan to loosen cake; remove rim. Top cheesecake with remaining berries.

Nutrition Information

- Calories: 290
- Total Carbohydrate: 25 g
- Fiber: 2 g
- Protein: 3 g
- Cholesterol: 65 mg
- Saturated Fat: 12 g
- Total Fat: 19 g
- Sodium: 220 mg
- Sugar: 19 g

7. Bird's Nest Mini Baked Cheesecakes

Serving: 12 | Prep: 20mins | Cook: 3hours20mins | Ready in: 3hours40mins

Ingredients

- 2 pkg. (8 oz. each) PHILADELPHIA Cream Cheese, softened
- 1/2 cup granulated sugar
- 1/2 tsp. vanilla
- 2 eggs
- 12 vanilla wafers
- 1 pkg. (4 oz.) BAKER'S Semi-Sweet Chocolate

- 1-1/2 cups chow mein noodles
- 36 JET-PUFFED Miniature Marshmallows
- 1 Tbsp. orange colored sugar

Direction

- Heat oven to 350°F.
- Beat cream cheese, granulated sugar and vanilla with mixer until blended. Add eggs, 1 at a time, beating on low speed after each just until blended.
- Place 1 wafer in each of 12 paper-lined muffin cups; cover with cream cheese batter.
- Bake 20 min. or until centers are almost set. Cool completely. Refrigerate 2 hours.
- Melt chocolate as directed on package; mix with noodles. Shape into 12 nests, using about 2 Tbsp. for each. Cut triangular piece from each marshmallow for the bird's beaks. Dip sticky sides of marshmallow wedges in sugar. Place 3 beaks in each nest. Place 1 nest on each cheesecake.

Nutrition Information

- Calories: 280
- Total Carbohydrate: 25 g
- Sugar: 17 g
- Saturated Fat: 10 g
- Protein: 5 g
- Fiber: 0 g
- Cholesterol: 75 mg
- Sodium: 220 mg
- Total Fat: 18 g

8. Bit Of Irish Cheesecake

Serving: 16 | Prep: 15mins | Cook: 6hours5mins | Ready in: 6hours20mins

Ingredients

- 1-1/2 cups finely chopped PLANTERS Pecans
- 2 Tbsp. sugar

- 3 Tbsp. butter or margarine, melted
- 4 pkg. (8 oz. each) PHILADELPHIA Cream Cheese, softened
- 1 cup sugar
- 3 Tbsp. flour
- 1 cup BREAKSTONE'S or KNUDSEN Sour Cream
- 1/4 cup Irish cream liqueur
- 4 eggs

Direction

- Heat oven to 325°F.
- Combine nuts, 2 Tbsp. sugar and butter; press onto bottom of 9-inch springform pan. Bake 10 min.
- Meanwhile, beat cream cheese, 1 cup sugar and flour in large bowl with mixer until blended. Add sour cream and liqueur; mix well. Add eggs, 1 at a time, mixing on low speed after each just until blended.
- Pour cream cheese batter over crust. Bake 1 hour 5 min. or until center is almost set. Run knife around rim of pan to loosen cake; cool before removing rim. Refrigerate cheesecake 4 hours.

Nutrition Information

- Calories: 440
- Cholesterol: 125 mg
- Total Carbohydrate: 20 g
- Fiber: 1 g
- Sugar: 17 g
- Saturated Fat: 16 g
- Protein: 7 g
- Sodium: 260 mg
- Total Fat: 34 g

9. Bite Size Salted Caramel Cheesecakes

Serving: 24 | Prep: 20mins | Cook: 2hours45mins | Ready in: 3hours5mins

Ingredients

- 1/2 cup graham cracker crumbs
- 1 Tbsp. brown sugar
- 3/4 tsp. kosher salt, divided
- 2 Tbsp. butter, melted
- 1-1/2 pkg. (8 oz. each) PHILADELPHIA Cream Cheese (12 oz.), softened
- 1/2 cup granulated sugar
- 1 egg
- 12 KRAFT Caramels
- 1 Tbsp. milk

Direction

- Heat oven to 325°F.
- Combine graham crumbs, brown sugar, 1/4 tsp. salt and butter; press onto bottoms of 24 paper-lined mini muffin cups.
- Beat cream cheese and granulated sugar in medium bowl with mixer until blended. Add egg; beat just until blended. Spoon into muffin cups, adding about 1 Tbsp. cream cheese batter to each.
- Bake 15 min. or until centers of cheesecakes are almost set. Cool completely. Refrigerate 1 hour.
- Place caramels in small heatproof bowl. Add milk and 1/4 tsp. of the remaining salt. Place over pan of boiling water, making sure boiling water does not touch bottom of bowl. Cook until caramels are completely melted and mixture is well blended, stirring frequently.
- Drizzle about 1 tsp. caramel sauce over each cheesecake; sprinkle with remaining salt. Refrigerate 1 hour.

Nutrition Information

- Calories: 110
- Total Carbohydrate: 11 g
- Fiber: 0 g
- Sugar: 9 g
- Sodium: 140 mg
- Cholesterol: 25 mg
- Total Fat: 7 g
- Saturated Fat: 4 g

- Protein: 2 g

10. Black Forest Cheesecake

Serving: 0 | Prep: 20mins | Cook: 1hours | Ready in: 1hours20mins

Ingredients

- 2 pkg. (21.4 oz. each) JELL-O No Bake Cherry Cheesecake Dessert
- 2/3 cup margarine, melted
- 1/4 cup sugar
- 2 Tbsp. water
- 6 squares BAKER'S Semi-Sweet Chocolate, divided
- 2-1/2 cups cold milk

Direction

- Mix Crust Mixes, margarine, sugar and water with fork until well blended. Press half of the crumb mixture firmly 1-1/2 inches up side of 9-inch springform pan. Press remaining crumb mixture firmly onto bottom of pan using bottom of a dry measuring cup.
- Microwave 4 squares of the chocolate in small microwavable bowl on HIGH 2 minutes or until almost melted. Stir until chocolate is completely melted; set aside. Pour milk into large bowl of electric mixer. Add Filling Mixes; beat on low speed until well blended. Beat on medium speed 3 minutes. Blend in melted chocolate. (Filling will be thick.) Spoon into crust. Refrigerate at least 1 hour or until firm.
- Melt remaining 2 oz. chocolate as directed on package just before serving. Spoon Cherry Topping onto cheesecake; drizzle with melted chocolate. Refrigerate 5 minutes to harden chocolate. Run small knife or spatula around rim of pan to loosen crust; remove rim of pan. Store leftover cheesecake in refrigerator.

Nutrition Information

- Calories: 380
- Cholesterol: 5 mg
- Total Carbohydrate: 59 g
- Total Fat: 16 g
- Sodium: 410 mg
- Protein: 4 g
- Fiber: 1 g
- Sugar: 38 g
- Saturated Fat: 6 g

11. Blossoming Berry Cheesecake

Serving: 0 | Prep: 25mins | Cook: 4hours55mins | Ready in: 5hours20mins

Ingredients

- 1 cup graham cracker crumbs
- 3 Tbsp. sugar
- 3 Tbsp. butter or margarine, melted
- 2 eggs, separated
- 2 pkg. (8 oz. each) PHILADELPHIA Cream Cheese, softened
- 1/2 cup sugar
- 1 tsp. grated lemon zest
- 1 Tbsp. lemon juice
- 1-1/2 tsp. vanilla, divided
- 1 cup BREAKSTONE'S or KNUDSEN Sour Cream
- 2 Tbsp. sugar
- 1 cup sliced strawberries
- 1/2 cup fresh raspberries

Direction

- Preheat oven to 325°F if using a silver 9-inch springform pan (or to 300°F if using a dark nonstick 9-inch springform pan). Mix crumbs, 3 Tbsp. sugar and butter; press firmly onto bottom of pan. Bake 10 minutes; set aside.
- Beat egg whites in small bowl with electric mixer on high speed until stiff peaks form; set aside. Beat cream cheese, 1/2 cup sugar,

lemon peel, juice and 1/2 tsp. of the vanilla in large bowl with electric mixer on medium speed until well blended. Add egg yolks, 1 at a time, mixing on low speed after each addition just until blended. Gently stir in egg whites; pour over crust.

- Bake 45 minutes or until center is almost set. Mix sour cream, 2 Tbsp. sugar and remaining 1 tsp. vanilla. Carefully spread over cheesecake. Bake an additional 10 minutes. Run small knife or metal spatula around rim of pan to loosen cake; cool before removing rim of pan. Refrigerate 4 hours or overnight. Top with strawberries and raspberries just before serving. Garnish with fresh mint, if desired. Store leftover cheesecake in refrigerator.

Nutrition Information

- Calories: 230
- Fiber: 1 g
- Sugar: 0 g
- Cholesterol: 75 mg
- Total Carbohydrate: 0 g
- Protein: 4 g
- Saturated Fat: 9 g
- Sodium: 180 mg
- Total Fat: 16 g

12. Blueberry Cheesecake Bars

Serving: 16 | Prep: 20mins | Cook: 3hours15mins | Ready in: 3hours35mins

Ingredients

- 2 cups graham cracker crumbs
- 1/3 cup butter, melted
- 2 pkg. (8 oz. each) PHILADELPHIA Cream Cheese, softened
- 3/4 cup sugar
- 1 tsp. vanilla
- 2 eggs
- 1 jar (10 oz.) blueberry preserves
- 1 cup blueberries

Direction

- Heat oven to 350°F.
- Combine graham crumbs and butter; press onto bottom of 13x9-inch pan. Refrigerate until ready to use.
- Beat cream cheese in large bowl with mixer until creamy. Add sugar and vanilla; mix well. Add eggs, 1 at a time, mixing on low speed after each just until blended.
- Stir preserves (in jar) until softened; spread evenly onto crust. Top with blueberries; cover with cream cheese mixture.
- Bake 30 min. or until slightly puffed. Cool completely. Refrigerate 2 hours before cutting into bars.

Nutrition Information

- Calories: 280
- Cholesterol: 65 mg
- Sugar: 0 g
- Protein: 3 g
- Sodium: 200 mg
- Total Carbohydrate: 0 g
- Total Fat: 15 g
- Saturated Fat: 9 g
- Fiber: 0.675 g

13. Butter Pecan Cheesecake

Serving: 12 | Prep: 45mins | Cook: 5hours55mins | Ready in: 6hours40mins

Ingredients

- 6 Tbsp. butter, divided
- 16 pecan shortbread cookies (2 inch), finely crushed (about 2 cups)
- 1 cup plus 3 Tbsp. brown sugar, divided
- 1/4 tsp. salt

- 1 pkg. (6 oz.) PLANTERS Pecan Halves
- 4 pkg. (8 oz. each) PHILADELPHIA Cream Cheese, softened
- 1 tsp. vanilla
- 4 eggs
- 10 KRAFT Caramels
- 3 Tbsp. half-and-half

Direction

- Heat oven to 325°F.
- Melt 1/4 cup (4 Tbsp.) butter in medium nonstick skillet on medium heat. Continue to cook 2 min. or until light golden brown in color with a nutty aroma, stirring constantly. Mix with cookie crumbs; press onto bottom and 1 inch up side of 9-inch springform pan.
- Bake 10 min. or until lightly browned.
- Meanwhile, melt remaining butter in same skillet. Add 3 Tbsp. sugar and salt; mix well. Cook and stir 1 to 2 min. or until sugar is dissolved. Stir in nuts; cook 5 min. or until nuts are lightly browned and evenly glazed, stirring constantly. Spread onto large sheet of parchment; cool.
- Beat cream cheese, vanilla and remaining sugar in large bowl with mixer until blended. Add eggs, 1 at a time, mixing on low speed after each just until blended. Pour half the batter over crust.
- Reserve 3/4 cup nuts for later use. Chop remaining nuts; sprinkle over batter. Cover with remaining batter.
- Bake 55 min. or until center is almost set. Run knife around rim of pan to loosen cake; cool before removing rim. Refrigerate cheesecake 4 hours.
- Microwave caramels and half-and-half in microwaveable bowl on HIGH 1 to 2 min. or until caramels are completely melted, stirring after each minute. Arrange reserved nuts on top of cheesecake; drizzle with caramel sauce.

Nutrition Information

- Calories: 650
- Saturated Fat: 23 g

- Cholesterol: 165 mg
- Sugar: 29 g
- Protein: 10 g
- Sodium: 500 mg
- Total Carbohydrate: 40 g
- Fiber: 2 g
- Total Fat: 51 g

14. Cappuccino Cheesecake

Serving: 0 | Prep: 25mins | Cook: 6hours10mins | Ready in: 6hours35mins

Ingredients

- 1-1/2 cups finely chopped PLANTERS Walnuts
- 3 Tbsp. butter or margarine, melted
- 2 Tbsp. sugar
- 1 Tbsp. MAXWELL HOUSE Instant Coffee
- 1/4 tsp. ground cinnamon
- 1/4 cup boiling water
- 4 pkg. (8 oz. each) PHILADELPHIA Cream Cheese, softened
- 1 cup sugar
- 3 Tbsp. flour
- 4 eggs
- 1 cup BREAKSTONE'S or KNUDSEN Sour Cream
- 1-1/2 cups thawed COOL WHIP Whipped Topping

Direction

- Heat oven to 325°F.
- Mix nuts, butter and 2 Tbsp. sugar; press onto bottom of 9-inch springform pan. Bake 10 min. Meanwhile, dissolve instant coffee with cinnamon in boiling water.
- Remove crust from oven. Increase oven temperature to 450°F. Beat cream cheese, 1 cup sugar and flour with mixer until well blended. Add eggs, 1 at a time, mixing on low speed after each just until blended. Blend in sour

cream. Gradually beat in coffee; pour over crust.

- Bake 10 min. Reduce oven temperature to 250°F. Bake 1 hour or until center is almost set. Run knife around rim of pan to loosen cake; cool before removing rim. Refrigerate 4 hours. Top with dollops of COOL WHIP. Garnish with a sprinkle of additional cinnamon, if desired.

Nutrition Information

- Calories: 420
- Total Carbohydrate: 21 g
- Cholesterol: 145 mg
- Sodium: 250 mg
- Fiber: 1 g
- Saturated Fat: 17 g
- Protein: 8 g
- Total Fat: 34 g
- Sugar: 17 g

15. Caramel Bourbon Cheesecake Bites

Serving: 0 | Prep: | Cook: | Ready in:

Ingredients

- 8 square shortbread cookies, finely crushed (about 1/2 cup)
- 1 Tbsp. butter, melted
- 1-1/2 pkg. (8 oz. each) PHILADELPHIA Cream Cheese (12 oz.), softened
- 1/2 cup packed brown sugar
- 1 Tbsp. plus 1 tsp. bourbon, divided
- 1 vanilla bean
- 1 egg
- 12 KRAFT Caramels
- 1 Tbsp. milk

Direction

- Heat oven to 325°F.

- Combine cookie crumbs and butter; press onto bottoms of 24 paper-lined mini muffin cups, adding about 1 tsp. crumb mixture to each cup.
- Beat cream cheese, sugar and 1 Tbsp. bourbon in large bowl with mixer until blended. Use sharp knife to gently split vanilla bean pod lengthwise in half. Scrape seeds into cream cheese mixture; mix well. Add egg; beat on low speed just until blended.
- Spoon cream cheese mixture into prepared muffin cups, adding about 1 Tbsp. batter to each cup.
- Bake 12 to 14 min. or until centers of cheesecakes are almost set. Cool completely. Refrigerate 1 hour.
- Microwave caramels and milk in microwaveable bowl on HIGH 1 min. or until caramels are completely melted, stirring every 30 sec. Stir in remaining bourbon. Drizzle about 1 tsp. caramel sauce over each cheesecake. Refrigerate 1 hour.

Nutrition Information

- Calories: 0 g
- Sodium: 0 g
- Saturated Fat: 0 g
- Cholesterol: 0 g
- Sugar: 0 g
- Fiber: 0 g
- Total Carbohydrate: 0 g
- Total Fat: 0 g
- Protein: 0 g

16. Caramel Pumpkin Mousse Tart

Serving: 10 | Prep: 30mins | Cook: 4hours15mins | Ready in: 4hours45mins

Ingredients

- 60 vanilla wafers, divided
- 1/2 cup butter, divided

- 1/3 cup chopped PLANTERS Pecans
- 2 Tbsp. brown sugar
- 1-3/4 tsp. pumpkin pie spice, divided
- 1 pkg. (8 oz.) PHILADELPHIA Cream Cheese, softened
- 1 cup canned pumpkin
- 1 pkg. (3.4 oz.) JELL-O Vanilla Flavor Instant Pudding
- 1/2 cup milk
- 1 cup thawed COOL WHIP Whipped Topping
- 12 KRAFT Caramels
- 1 Tbsp. water

Direction

- Heat oven to 350°F.
- Crush 50 wafers to form fine crumbs; place in medium bowl. Melt 1/3 cup butter. Add to wafer crumbs; mix well. Press onto bottom of 9-1/2-inch tart pan.
- Crush remaining wafers coarsely; place in medium bowl. Melt remaining butter. Add to wafer crumbs along with the nuts, sugar and 1/4 tsp. pumpkin pie spice; mix well. Spread onto bottom of shallow pan; place in oven along with the crust.
- Bake crust and nut mixture 10 to 12 min. or until lightly browned; cool.
- Beat cream cheese and pumpkin in medium bowl with mixer until blended. Add dry pudding mix and remaining pie spice; beat until blended. Gradually beat in milk; spread over crust. Top with COOL WHIP, spreading to within 1/2 inch of edge. Refrigerate 4 hours. Meanwhile, break cooled baked nut mixture into smaller pieces; store in airtight container until ready to use.
- Remove tart from side of pan just before serving; top tart with nut mixture. Microwave caramels and water in microwaveable bowl on HIGH 1-1/2 min. or until caramels are completely melted, stirring after 45 sec. Drizzle over tart.

Nutrition Information

- Calories: 420
- Fiber: 2 g
- Cholesterol: 55 mg
- Sodium: 460 mg
- Saturated Fat: 14 g
- Total Fat: 26 g
- Protein: 4 g
- Sugar: 27 g
- Total Carbohydrate: 45 g

17. Centennial Cheesecake

Serving: 0 | Prep: 25mins | Cook: 1hours50mins | Ready in: 2hours15mins

Ingredients

- 4 pkg. (8 oz. each) PHILADELPHIA Cream Cheese, softened, divided
- 1/2 cup (1 stick) butter or margarine, softened
- 1-1/2 cups flour
- 1-1/4 cups plus 1 tsp. sugar, divided
- 1 Tbsp. grated lemon zest, divided
- 2 Tbsp. flour
- 1 Tbsp. lemon juice
- 4 eggs
- 1 can (21 oz.) cherry pie filling

Direction

- Beat 1 pkg. of the cream cheese and the butter in small bowl with electric mixer on medium speed until well blended. Add 1-1/2 cups flour, 1/4 cup of the sugar and 1 tsp. of the lemon zest; mix well. Shape into ball; cover. Refrigerate 1 hour or until chilled.
- Preheat oven to 375°F. Remove 1/4 cup of the dough; roll out to 1/8-inch thickness on lightly floured surface. Cut into desired shapes with lightly floured 1-inch cookie cutters. Sprinkle with 1 tsp. of the remaining sugar; place, 2 inches apart, on ungreased baking sheets. Bake 8 to 10 min. or until edges are very lightly browned. Remove to wire racks; cool completely. Meanwhile, spread 2/3 of the remaining dough onto bottom of 9-inch

springform pan. (Reduce oven to 350°F if using a dark nonstick springform pan.) Bake 25 min.; cool. Press remaining dough 2 inches up side of pan. Reduce oven temperature to 300°F (or to 275°F if using a dark pan).

- Beat remaining 3 pkg. cream cheese, remaining 1 cup sugar, remaining 2 tsp. peel, the 2 Tbsp. flour and lemon juice with electric mixer on medium speed until well blended. Add eggs, 1 at a time, mixing just until blended after each addition. Pour into crust.
- Bake 1 hour and 15 min. or until center is almost set. Run small knife or metal spatula around rim of pan to loosen cake; cool before removing rim of pan. Refrigerate 4 hours or overnight. Top with the pie filling and cutouts just before serving. Store leftover cheesecake in refrigerator.

Nutrition Information

- Calories: 420
- Protein: 7 g
- Cholesterol: 130 mg
- Total Carbohydrate: 0 g
- Fiber: 1 g
- Saturated Fat: 16 g
- Sodium: 290 mg
- Sugar: 0 g
- Total Fat: 27 g

18. Cheesecake Fruit Dip

Serving: 0 | Prep: 10mins | Cook: 1hours | Ready in: 1hours10mins

Ingredients

- 1/2 cup raspberries
- 1 tub (8 oz.) PHILADELPHIA Strawberry 1/3 Less Fat than Cream Cheese
- 2 tsp. orange juice

Direction

- Mash raspberries in medium bowl.
- Add remaining ingredients; mix well.
- Refrigerate 1 hour.

Nutrition Information

- Calories: 60
- Sugar: 0 g
- Fiber: 1 g
- Saturated Fat: 2 g
- Protein: 1 g
- Cholesterol: 10 mg
- Sodium: 80 mg
- Total Carbohydrate: 0 g
- Total Fat: 3.5 g

19. Cheesecake Topper

Serving: 0 | Prep: 10mins | Cook: | Ready in: 10mins

Ingredients

- 1 pkg. (8 oz.) PHILADELPHIA Neufchatel Cheese, softened
- 1/4 cup sugar
- 1 cup thawed COOL WHIP LITE Whipped Topping
- 10 graham crackers, broken in half (20 squares)
- 1-1/2 cups fresh raspberries

Direction

- Beat Neufchatel cheese and sugar in large bowl with wire whisk or electric mixer on medium speed until well blended. Stir in whipped topping.
- Spread 1 Tbsp. of the Neufchatel mixture onto each graham square just before serving.
- Top with raspberries.

Nutrition Information

- Calories: 80
- Cholesterol: 10 mg

- Fiber: 1 g
- Saturated Fat: 2.5 g
- Sodium: 95 mg
- Total Carbohydrate: 0 g
- Total Fat: 4 g
- Sugar: 0 g
- Protein: 2 g

20. Cherry Cheesecake

Serving: 8 | Prep: 10mins | Cook: 3hours | Ready in: 3hours10mins

Ingredients

- 1 pkg. (8 oz.) PHILADELPHIA Cream Cheese, softened
- 1/3 cup sugar
- 1 tub (8 oz.) COOL WHIP Whipped Topping, thawed
- 1 ready-to-use graham cracker crumb crust (6 oz.)
- 1-1/2 cups cherry pie filling

Direction

- Beat cream cheese and sugar in large bowl with whisk or mixer until blended. Stir in COOL WHIP.
- Spoon into crust.
- Refrigerate 3 hours. Serve topped with cherry pie filling.

Nutrition Information

- Calories: 360
- Total Fat: 20 g
- Sugar: 0 g
- Sodium: 250 mg
- Total Carbohydrate: 0 g
- Saturated Fat: 12 g
- Cholesterol: 30 mg
- Protein: 3 g
- Fiber: 0.5865 g

21. Cherry Cheesecake Recipe

Serving: 12 | Prep: 15mins | Cook: 5hours45mins | Ready in: 6hours

Ingredients

- 2 chocolate graham crackers, crushed
- 2 cups BREAKSTONE'S or KNUDSEN 2% Milkfat Low Fat Cottage Cheese
- 1 pkg. (8 oz.) PHILADELPHIA Neufchatel Cheese, cubed, softened
- 1/2 cup plain nonfat yogurt
- 3 Tbsp. sugar, divided
- 2 Tbsp. flour
- 1 tsp. vanilla
- 1 whole egg
- 2 egg whites
- 1 cup drained canned pitted tart cherries in water with 1/3 cup liquid reserved, divided
- 2 tsp. MINUTE Tapioca

Direction

- Heat oven to 325ºF.
- Sprinkle graham crumbs onto bottom of 9-inch springform pan.
- Process cottage cheese in food processor until smooth. Add Neufchatel, yogurt, 2 Tbsp. sugar, flour and vanilla; process until blended. Add whole egg and egg whites, 1 at a time, pulsing after each just until blended. Pour into springform pan.
- Bake 40 to 45 min. or until center is almost set. Run knife around rim of pan to loosen cake; cool before removing rim. Refrigerate cheesecake 4 hours. Meanwhile, bring reserved cherry liquid, tapioca and remaining sugar to boil in large saucepan on medium-high heat, stirring constantly. Simmer on medium-low heat 2 min. or until thickened, stirring constantly. Remove from heat. Gently stir in cherries. Cool, then refrigerate until ready to use.

- Spoon cherry sauce over cheesecake just before serving.

Nutrition Information

- Calories: 130
- Cholesterol: 35 mg
- Fiber: 0 g
- Total Carbohydrate: 0 g
- Total Fat: 6 g
- Sodium: 240 mg
- Sugar: 0 g
- Saturated Fat: 3.5 g
- Protein: 7 g

22. Chocolate Cheesecake Flan

Serving: 12 | Prep: 20mins | Cook: 6hours | Ready in: 6hours20mins

Ingredients

- 1-1/2 pkg. (4 oz. each) BAKER'S Semi-Sweet Chocolate (6 oz.), divided
- 1-1/2 cups sugar, divided
- 1 can (12 oz.) evaporated milk
- 1 pkg. (8 oz.) PHILADELPHIA Cream Cheese, cubed, softened
- 4 egg s

Direction

- Heat oven to 350°F.
- Melt 4 oz. chocolate as directed on package; cool. Meanwhile, cook 1 cup sugar in saucepan on medium heat until deep golden brown, stirring constantly. Pour into 9-inch round pan.
- Blend milk and cream cheese in blender until smooth. Add eggs, remaining sugar and melted chocolate; blend well. Pour over syrup in pan; place filled pan in larger pan. Add enough water to larger pan to come halfway up side of filled pan.

- Bake 1 hour or until knife inserted in center comes out clean. Remove flan from water-filled pan; cool completely. Refrigerate 4 hours.
- Meanwhile, melt remaining chocolate. Use teaspoon to drizzle chocolate into 5 or 6 designs on sheet of waxed paper; let stand until firm.
- Loosen flan from side of pan just before serving; unmold onto plate. Carefully remove chocolate designs from waxed paper; use to garnish flan.

Nutrition Information

- Calories: 290
- Fiber: 1 g
- Total Carbohydrate: 37 g
- Sugar: 34 g
- Cholesterol: 95 mg
- Saturated Fat: 8 g
- Protein: 6 g
- Total Fat: 14 g
- Sodium: 125 mg

23. Chocolate Cheesecake Ice Cream Cake

Serving: 16 | Prep: 15mins | Cook: 4hours | Ready in: 4hours15mins

Ingredients

- 2 pkg. (8 oz. each) PHILADELPHIA Cream Cheese, softened
- 2 oz. BAKER'S Semi-Sweet Chocolate, melted, cooled
- 1/2 cup sugar
- 2 tsp. vanilla
- 6 cups chocolate ice cream, slightly softened
- 1 pkg. (14.3 oz.) vanilla creme-filled chocolate sandwich cookies, divided

Direction

- Beat cream cheese, chocolate, sugar and vanilla in large bowl with mixer until blended. Add ice cream; mix well. Spoon into foil-lined 2-qt. bowl; spread to form even layer on top.
- Crush 20 cookies to form fine crumbs; sprinkle evenly over cream cheese mixture. Press gently into cream cheese mixture to secure.
- Freeze 4 hours or until firm. Meanwhile, chop remaining cookies.
- Unmold dessert onto plate just before serving. Remove and discard foil. Press chopped cookies into dessert.

Nutrition Information

- Calories: 370
- Total Fat: 21 g
- Sugar: 0 g
- Protein: 5 g
- Saturated Fat: 11 g
- Cholesterol: 55 mg
- Fiber: 2 g
- Total Carbohydrate: 0 g
- Sodium: 260 mg

24. Chocolate Mint Cookie Cheesecake

Serving: 16 | Prep: 30mins | Cook: 6hours | Ready in: 6hours30mins

Ingredients

- 32 chocolate-covered mint cookies, divided
- 2 Tbsp. butter or margarine, melted
- 7 oz. BAKER'S Semi-Sweet Chocolate, divided
- 4 pkg. (8 oz. each) PHILADELPHIA Cream Cheese, softened
- 3/4 cup sugar
- 1 tsp. vanilla
- 3/4 tsp. peppermint extract
- 4 eggs

Direction

- Heat oven to 325°F.
- Reserve 1 cookie for garnish. Finely crush remaining cookies; mix with butter until blended. Press onto bottom of 9-inch springform pan.
- Melt 6 oz. chocolate as directed on package. Beat cream cheese, sugar, vanilla and peppermint extract with mixer until blended. Add melted chocolate; mix well. Add eggs, 1 at a time, mixing on low speed after each just until blended. Pour over crust.
- Bake 55 min. to 1 hour or until center is almost set. Run knife around rim of pan to loosen cake; cool before removing rim. Refrigerate cheesecake 4 hours.
- Melt remaining chocolate; drizzle over cake. Garnish with reserved cookie.

Nutrition Information

- Calories: 400
- Total Fat: 29 g
- Sugar: 0 g
- Protein: 7 g
- Saturated Fat: 17 g
- Total Carbohydrate: 0 g
- Fiber: 1 g
- Sodium: 290 mg
- Cholesterol: 125 mg

25. Chocolate Truffle Cheesecake

Serving: 16 | Prep: 20mins | Cook: 5hours10mins | Ready in: 5hours30mins

Ingredients

- 18 OREO Cookies, finely crushed
- 2 Tbsp. butter or margarine, melted
- 3 pkg. (8 oz. each) PHILADELPHIA Cream Cheese, softened
- 1 can (14 oz.) sweetened condensed milk
- 2 tsp. vanilla

- 3 pkg. (4 oz. each) BAKER'S Semi-Sweet Chocolate, melted, slightly cooled
- 4 eggs

Direction

- Heat oven to 300°F.
- Combine cookie crumbs and butter; press onto bottom of 9-inch springform pan.
- Beat cream cheese, sweetened condensed milk and vanilla in large bowl with mixer until blended. Add melted chocolate; mix well. Add eggs, 1 at a time, mixing on low speed after each just until blended. Pour over crust.
- Bake 1 hour 5 min. to 1 hour 10 min. or until center is almost set. Run knife around rim of pan to loosen cake; cool before removing rim. Refrigerate cheesecake 4 hours.

Nutrition Information

- Calories: 420
- Sugar: 0 g
- Saturated Fat: 16 g
- Cholesterol: 115 mg
- Fiber: 2 g
- Protein: 8 g
- Total Fat: 28 g
- Sodium: 280 mg
- Total Carbohydrate: 0 g

26. Chocolate Velvet Cheesecake

Serving: 0 | Prep: 30mins | Cook: 4hours45mins | Ready in: 5hours15mins

Ingredients

- 38 OREO Cookies, divided
- 5 Tbsp. butter or margarine, melted
- 5 oz. BAKER'S Semi-Sweet Chocolate, divided
- 1 pkg. (8 oz.) PHILADELPHIA Cream Cheese, softened
- 1/2 cup plus 2 Tbsp. sugar, divided

- 1-1/2 cups BREAKSTONE'S or KNUDSEN Sour Cream, divided
- 1 tsp. vanilla
- 2 eggs

Direction

- Preheat oven to 325°F. Crush 24 of the cookies until fine crumbs form; mix with butter until well blended. Press firmly onto bottom of 9-inch springform pan. Stand remaining 14 cookies around edge of pan, pressing into crumb mixture to secure. Set aside. Place 4 oz. chocolate in small saucepan; cook on low heat until melted, stirring frequently. Set aside.
- Beat cream cheese and 1/2 cup of the sugar in large bowl with electric mixer on medium speed until well blended. Add melted chocolate, 1/2 cup of the sour cream and the vanilla; mix well. Add eggs, 1 at a time, mixing just until blended after each addition. Pour into prepared crust.
- Bake 35 to 40 min. or until center is almost set. Combine remaining 1 cup sour cream and remaining 2 Tbsp. sugar; spread over cheesecake. Bake an additional 5 min. Cool. Melt remaining chocolate as directed on pkg.; drizzle over cheesecake. Refrigerate at least 4 hours. Store leftover cheesecake in refrigerator.

Nutrition Information

- Calories: 380
- Total Carbohydrate: 0 g
- Protein: 5 g
- Cholesterol: 75 mg
- Saturated Fat: 12 g
- Sugar: 0 g
- Total Fat: 25 g
- Sodium: 300 mg
- Fiber: 2 g

27. Chocolate Orange Cheesecake

Serving: 16 | Prep: 20mins | Cook: 6hours | Ready in: 6hours20mins

Ingredients

- 20 chocolate wafer cookies, finely crushed (about 1 cup)
- 1/4 tsp. ground cinnamon
- 3 Tbsp. butter, melted
- 4 pkg. (8 oz. each) PHILADELPHIA Cream Cheese, softened
- 3/4 cup sugar
- 1/2 cup BREAKSTONE'S or KNUDSEN Sour Cream
- 1 tsp. vanilla
- 4 eggs
- 1 pkg. (4 oz.) BAKER'S Semi-Sweet Chocolate, melted
- 2 Tbsp. orange-flavored liqueur
- 1 tsp. orange zest
- 1/2 cup orange marmalade

Direction

- Heat oven to 350°F.
- Combine wafer crumbs, cinnamon and butter; press onto bottom of 9-inch springform pan.
- Beat cream cheese and sugar in large bowl with mixer until blended. Add sour cream and vanilla; mix well. Add eggs, 1 at a time, mixing on low speed after each just until blended. Transfer 3 cups batter to medium bowl; stir in melted chocolate. Pour over crust.
- Bake 30 min. Meanwhile, stir liqueur and orange zest into remaining batter; refrigerate until ready to use.
- Reduce oven temperature to 325°F. Spoon remaining batter over baked chocolate layer in pan; bake 30 min. or until center is almost set. Run small knife around rim of pan to loosen cake; cool before removing rim. Refrigerate cheesecake 4 hours.
- Heat marmalade just until warmed; spoon over cheesecake just before serving.

Nutrition Information

- Calories: 380
- Sodium: 310 mg
- Total Carbohydrate: 0 g
- Protein: 6 g
- Fiber: 1 g
- Total Fat: 27 g
- Cholesterol: 130 mg
- Sugar: 0 g
- Saturated Fat: 16 g

28. Chocolate Orange Cheesecake Layer Cake

Serving: 16 | Prep: 30mins | Cook: 5hours45mins | Ready in: 6hours15mins

Ingredients

- 1 pkg. (2-layer size) chocolate cake mix
- 1 pkg. (3.9 oz.) JELL-O Chocolate Flavor Instant Pudding
- 3-1/2 pkg. (8 oz. each) PHILADELPHIA Cream Cheese (28 oz.), softened, divided
- 3/4 cup sugar
- 2 tsp. vanilla, divided
- 3/4 cup BREAKSTONE'S or KNUDSEN Sour Cream
- 3 eggs
- 2 tsp. finely chopped orange peel
- 1/4 cup orange marmalade
- 1 jar (7 oz.) JET-PUFFED Marshmallow Creme
- 1 tub (8 oz.) COOL WHIP Whipped Topping, thawed
- 1/2 oz. BAKER'S Semi-Sweet Chocolate, coarsely grated

Direction

- Heat oven to 325°F.
- Fold 2 (16-inch-long) sheets of foil lengthwise in half twice to form 3-inch-wide strips. Place 1 in each of 2 (9-inch) round pans, with ends of foil extending over sides. Spray with cooking

spray. Prepare cake batter as directed on package. Add dry pudding mix; beat 2 min. Pour into prepared pans.

- Bake 25 min. or until toothpick inserted in centers comes out clean. Remove cakes from oven; flatten tops with back of spatula. Beat 3 pkg. cream cheese, sugar and 1 tsp. vanilla in large bowl with mixer until blended. Add sour cream; mix well. Add eggs, 1 at a time, mixing on low speed after each just until blended. Stir in orange peel.
- Pour cheesecake batter evenly over cakes. Return to oven. Bake 25 to 30 min. or until centers of cheesecakes are almost set. Run knife around rims of pans to loosen cakes; cool completely. Refrigerate 4 hours. Use foil handles to remove cakes from pans. Place 1 cake layer on serving plate. Microwave marmalade in microwaveable bowl on HIGH 20 sec.; stir. Spread over cake layer on plate; top with remaining cake layer.
- Beat remaining cream cheese, remaining vanilla and marshmallow creme in large bowl with mixer until blended. Add COOL WHIP; beat on low speed just until blended. Spread onto top and side of cake. Sprinkle with grated chocolate.

Nutrition Information

- Calories: 520
- Total Fat: 29 g
- Fiber: 0.9579 g
- Total Carbohydrate: 58 g
- Sugar: 42 g
- Cholesterol: 130 mg
- Sodium: 550 mg
- Protein: 7 g
- Saturated Fat: 16 g

29. Cinnamon Streusel Pumpkin Cheesecake Bars

Serving: 24 | Prep: 20mins | Cook: 5hours40mins | Ready in: 6hours

Ingredients

- 3 cups flour
- 1-1/2 cups packed brown sugar, divided
- 1 Tbsp. ground cinnamon
- 1 cup butter, melted
- 3 pkg. (8 oz. each) PHILADELPHIA Cream Cheese, softened
- 1 cup canned pumpkin
- 1 tsp. vanilla
- 1-1/2 tsp. pumpkin pie spice
- 3 eggs
- 1 Tbsp. powdered sugar

Direction

- Heat oven to 350°F.
- Line 13x9-inch pan with foil, with ends of foil extending over sides. Spray with cooking spray.
- Combine flour, 1 cup brown sugar, cinnamon and butter. Reserve 1-1/2 cups flour mixture for later use; press remaining flour mixture onto bottom of prepared pan. Bake 20 min.
- Meanwhile, beat cream cheese and remaining brown sugar in large bowl with mixer until blended. Add pumpkin, vanilla and pumpkin pie spice; mix well. Add eggs, 1 at a time, mixing on low speed after each just until blended.
- Pour cream cheese mixture over crust; sprinkle with reserved flour mixture.
- Bake 35 to 40 min. or until center is almost set. Cool completely.
- Refrigerate 4 hours. Sprinkle with powdered sugar just before serving. Use foil handles to remove dessert from pan before cutting into bars.

Nutrition Information

- Calories: 300
- Total Fat: 18 g
- Sodium: 180 mg
- Protein: 5 g
- Fiber: 1 g
- Cholesterol: 75 mg
- Sugar: 0 g
- Total Carbohydrate: 0 g
- Saturated Fat: 11 g

30. Citrus Gelatin Layered Cheesecake

Serving: 16 | Prep: 15mins | Cook: 4hours30mins | Ready in: 4hours45mins

Ingredients

- 1-1/2 cups graham cracker crumbs
- 1/2 cup plus 2 Tbsp. sugar, divided
- 1/4 cup butter, melted
- 2 pkg. (8 oz. each) PHILADELPHIA Cream Cheese, softened
- 1/2 cup BREAKSTONE'S or KNUDSEN Sour Cream
- 2 eggs
- 3 navel oranges, divided
- 2 pkg. (3 oz. each) JELL-O Lemon Flavor Gelatin

Direction

- Heat oven to 325°F.
- Mix graham crumbs, 2 Tbsp. sugar and butter; press onto bottom of 9-inch springform pan.
- Beat cream cheese and remaining sugar with mixer until blended. Blend in sour cream. Add eggs, 1 at a time, beating on low speed after each just until blended. Zest 1 orange; stir zest into batter. (Reserve orange for later use). Pour batter over crust.
- Bake 45 min. or until center is almost set. Cool completely. Meanwhile, prepare gelatin as directed on package. Refrigerate 30 min. or until slightly thickened.

- Remove peels from oranges; cut into 1/4-inch-thick slices. Arrange in circular pattern on top of cheesecake, overlapping slices slightly; cover with 1/3 cup gelatin. Refrigerate 15 min. or until almost set. Spoon remaining gelatin over cheesecake. Refrigerate 2 hours or until firm. Run knife around rim of pan to loosen cake before removing rim.

Nutrition Information

- Calories: 270
- Total Carbohydrate: 0 g
- Total Fat: 15 g
- Cholesterol: 75 mg
- Fiber: 1 g
- Sodium: 260 mg
- Sugar: 0 g
- Saturated Fat: 9 g
- Protein: 4 g

31. Coconut Lime Cheesecake

Serving: 16 | Prep: 25mins | Cook: 6hours15mins | Ready in: 6hours40mins

Ingredients

- 30 square shortbread cookies, finely crushed (about 2 cups)
- 3/4 cup BAKER'S ANGEL FLAKE Coconut, divided
- 3 Tbsp. butter, melted
- 4 pkg. (8 oz. each) PHILADELPHIA Cream Cheese, softened
- 1 cup sugar
- 3/4 cup BREAKSTONE'S or KNUDSEN Sour Cream
- Zest and juice from 2 limes
- 4 eggs
- 3/4 cup thawed COOL WHIP Whipped Topping

Direction

- Heat oven to 325°F.
- Mix cookie crumbs, 1/2 cup coconut and butter; press onto bottom of 9-inch springform pan. Bake 10 to 12 min. or until lightly browned. Meanwhile, spread remaining coconut onto bottom of microwaveable pie plate. Microwave on HIGH 2 min. or until lightly toasted, stirring every 30 sec.
- Beat cream cheese and sugar in large bowl with mixer until blended. Add sour cream, lime zest and juice; mix well. Add eggs, 1 at a time, mixing on low speed after each just until blended. Pour over crust.
- Bake 1 to 1-1/4 hours or until center is almost set. Run knife around rim of pan to loosen cake. Cool before removing rim. Refrigerate cheesecake 4 hours.
- Serve topped with COOL WHIP and toasted coconut.

Nutrition Information

- Calories: 540
- Sodium: 450 mg
- Saturated Fat: 23 g
- Sugar: 0 g
- Fiber: 1 g
- Protein: 8 g
- Cholesterol: 180 mg
- Total Carbohydrate: 0 g
- Total Fat: 40 g

32. Coconut Strawberry Banana Bars

Serving: 24 | Prep: 30mins | Cook: 1hours45mins | Ready in: 2hours15mins

Ingredients

- 1/2 cup butter, softened
- 1 pkg. (2-layer size) coconut cake mix
- 2 eggs, divided

- 1 pkg. (8 oz.) PHILADELPHIA Cream Cheese, softened
- 1/3 cup granulated sugar
- 1 tsp. almond extract
- 1 large banana, sliced
- 2 cups sliced fresh strawberries
- 1/4 cup BAKER'S ANGEL FLAKE Coconut, toasted
- 1 tsp. powdered sugar

Direction

- Heat oven to 350°F.
- Beat butter, cake mix and 1 egg in large bowl with mixer until crumbly. Reserve 3/4 cup crumb mixture; press remaining onto bottom of 13x9-inch pan sprayed with cooking spray. Bake 10 min.
- Meanwhile, beat cream cheese, granulated sugar and almond extract until blended. Add remaining egg; mix well.
- Place banana slices over crust; cover with cream cheese mixture. Top with strawberries, coconut and reserved crumb mixture.
- Bake 45 min. or until center is set and crumb topping is lightly browned. Cool completely. Refrigerate 30 min. before cutting into bars.
- Garnish with sifted powdered sugar just before serving.

Nutrition Information

- Calories: 190
- Total Fat: 10 g
- Cholesterol: 40 mg
- Sodium: 210 mg
- Total Carbohydrate: 0 g
- Sugar: 0 g
- Saturated Fat: 5 g
- Fiber: 1 g
- Protein: 2 g

33. Coffee Cheesecake Pie

Serving: 10 | Prep: 15mins | Cook: 4hours40mins | Ready in: 4hours55mins

Ingredients

- 2 pkg. (8 oz. each) PHILADELPHIA Cream Cheese, softened
- 1/2 cup sugar
- 2 eggs
- 1/3 cup freshly brewed strong MAXWELL HOUSE Coffee, any variety, at room temperature
- 1 OREO Pie Crust (6 oz.)
- 1 oz. BAKER'S Semi-Sweet Chocolate
- Coffee-Caramel Sauce

Direction

- Heat oven to 350°F.
- Beat cream cheese and sugar in large bowl with mixer until blended. Add eggs and coffee; mix just until blended. Pour into crust.
- Bake 35 to 40 min. or until center is almost set. Cool completely.
- Refrigerate 3 hours. Melt chocolate as directed on package; drizzle over pie. Serve topped with Coffee-Caramel Sauce.

Nutrition Information

- Calories: 390
- Total Fat: 21 g
- Sodium: 350 mg
- Sugar: 0 g
- Fiber: 1 g
- Saturated Fat: 11 g
- Cholesterol: 105 mg
- Total Carbohydrate: 0 g
- Protein: 6 g

34. Creamy No Bake Chocolate Pudding Cheesecake

Serving: 10 | Prep: 15mins | Cook: 1hours | Ready in: 1hours15mins

Ingredients

- 1 pkg. (3.9 oz.) JELL-O Chocolate Flavor Instant Pudding
- 1-1/4 cups cold milk
- 2 pkg. (8 oz. each) PHILADELPHIA Cream Cheese, softened
- 1/4 cup sugar
- 1-1/2 cups thawed COOL WHIP Whipped Topping, divided
- 1 OREO Pie Crust (6 oz.)
- 1 oz. BAKER'S Semi-Sweet Chocolate

Direction

- Beat pudding mix and milk in medium bowl with whisk 2 min.
- Beat cream cheese and sugar in large bowl with mixer until blended. Gradually add pudding, beating well after each addition. Gently stir in 1 cup COOL WHIP. Spoon into crust.
- Refrigerate 4 hours.
- Meanwhile, melt semi-sweet chocolate as directed on package, then brush a 2-inch wide strip onto a piece of parchment paper. Refrigerate until firm.
- Break chocolate into pieces. Top cheesecake with remaining COOL WHIP and chocolate pieces just before serving.

Nutrition Information

- Calories: 350
- Saturated Fat: 14 g
- Sugar: 0 g
- Cholesterol: 65 mg
- Protein: 5 g
- Sodium: 440 mg
- Fiber: 1 g
- Total Fat: 23 g

- Total Carbohydrate: 0 g

35. Cupid's Cherry Cheesecakes

Serving: 12 | Prep: 15mins | Cook: 2hours30mins | Ready in: 2hours45mins

Ingredients

- 12 vanilla wafers
- 2 pkg. (8 oz. each) PHILADELPHIA Cream Cheese, softened
- 3/4 cup sugar
- 2 eggs
- 3/4 cup cherry pie filling

Direction

- Heat oven to 350°F.
- Place 1 wafer in each of 12 paper-lined muffin cups.
- Beat cream cheese and sugar in small bowl with mixer until light and fluffy. Add eggs, 1 at a time, mixing after each addition just until blended. Spoon over wafers in muffin cups.
- Bake 30 min. Turn off oven; open oven door slightly. Let stand in oven 30 min. Remove from oven; cool completely. Top with pie filling.
- Refrigerate 1 hour.

Nutrition Information

- Calories: 220
- Fiber: 0 g
- Sodium: 170 mg
- Cholesterol: 80 mg
- Saturated Fat: 8 g
- Total Carbohydrate: 0 g
- Sugar: 0 g
- Protein: 4 g
- Total Fat: 14 g

36. Double Lemon Cheesecake

Serving: 0 | Prep: 35mins | Cook: 5hours25mins | Ready in: 6hours

Ingredients

- 1 cup finely crushed vanilla wafers
- 3 Tbsp. sugar
- 3 Tbsp. butter or margarine, melted
- 4 eggs, divided
- 3 pkg. (8 oz. each) PHILADELPHIA Cream Cheese, softened
- 1 cup sugar
- 3 Tbsp. flour
- 1 Tbsp. grated lemon zest
- 2 Tbsp. lemon juice
- 1/2 tsp. vanilla
- 3/4 cup sugar
- 2 Tbsp. cornstarch
- 1/4 cup lemon juice

Direction

- Preheat oven to 325°F if using a silver 9-inch springform pan (or to 300°F if using a dark nonstick 9-inch springform pan). Mix crumbs, 3 Tbsp. sugar and the butter; press firmly onto bottom of pan. Bake 10 min.
- Separate one of the eggs. Cover and refrigerate egg yolk for later use. Set egg white aside. Beat cream cheese, 1 cup sugar, the flour, lemon zest, 2 Tbsp. lemon juice and the vanilla in large bowl with electric mixer on medium speed until well blended. Add egg white and remaining 3 whole eggs, one at a time, mixing on low speed after each addition just until blended. Pour over crust.
- Bake 50 to 55 min. or until center is almost set. Run knife or metal spatula around rim of pan to loosen cake; cool before removing rim of pan. Refrigerate 4 hours or overnight.
- Mix 3/4 cup sugar and cornstarch in medium saucepan; gradually stir in 1/2 cup water and 1/4 cup juice until well blended. Bring just to boil on medium heat, stirring constantly; cook

and stir until clear and thickened. Beat reserved egg yolk lightly with fork. Stir in 2 Tbsp. of the hot cornstarch mixture. Return to remaining cornstarch mixture in saucepan; mix until well blended. Cook 1 min. or until thickened, stirring constantly. Cool slightly. Spoon glaze over cheesecake. Refrigerate until set.

Nutrition Information

- Calories: 320
- Sugar: 0 g
- Fiber: 0 g
- Total Fat: 19 g
- Total Carbohydrate: 0 g
- Saturated Fat: 12 g
- Cholesterol: 105 mg
- Sodium: 240 mg
- Protein: 5 g

37. Double Decker OREO Cheesecake

Serving: 16 | Prep: 25mins | Cook: 5hours45mins | Ready in: 6hours10mins

Ingredients

- 1 pkg. (15.25 oz.) OREO Chocolate Creme Cookies, divided
- 1/4 cup butter, melted
- 4 pkg. (8 oz. each) PHILADELPHIA Cream Cheese, softened
- 1 cup sugar
- 1 tsp. vanilla
- 1 cup BREAKSTONE'S or KNUDSEN Sour Cream
- 4 eggs
- 1 pkg. (4 oz.) BAKER'S Semi-Sweet Chocolate, melted

Direction

- Heat oven to 325°F.
- Process 30 cookies in food processor until finely ground. Add butter; mix well. Press onto bottom of 13x9-inch pan.
- Beat cream cheese, sugar and vanilla in large bowl with mixer until blended. Add sour cream; mix well. Add eggs, 1 at a time, beating after each just until blended; pour half over crust. Stir melted chocolate into remaining batter; pour over batter in pan. Chop remaining cookies; sprinkle over batter.
- Bake 45 min. or until center is almost set. Cool completely. Refrigerate 4 hours.

Nutrition Information

- Calories: 490
- Sugar: 30 g
- Protein: 7 g
- Fiber: 2 g
- Cholesterol: 125 mg
- Total Fat: 34 g
- Saturated Fat: 19 g
- Total Carbohydrate: 39 g
- Sodium: 360 mg

38. Dulce De Leche Swirl Cheesecake

Serving: 16 | Prep: 15mins | Cook: 5hours45mins | Ready in: 6hours

Ingredients

- 1-1/2 cups graham cracker crumbs
- 1/4 cup butter, melted
- 3/4 cup plus 2 Tbsp. sugar, divided
- 4 pkg. (8 oz. each) PHILADELPHIA Cream Cheese, softened
- 1 cup BREAKSTONE'S or KNUDSEN Sour Cream
- 4 eggs
- 1 can (13.4 oz) dulce de leche (sweetened milk caramel)

Direction

- Heat oven to 325°F.
- Mix crumbs, butter and 2 Tbsp. sugar; press onto bottom of 9-inch springform pan.
- Beat cream cheese and remaining sugar in large bowl with mixer until well blended. Add sour cream; mix well. Add eggs, 1 at a time, mixing on low speed after each just until blended.
- Remove 1-1/4 cups cheesecake batter; mix with dulce de leche. Pour remaining batter over crust. Gently drop spoonfuls of caramel mixture over batter; swirl gently with knife.
- Bake 1 hour 15 min. or until center is almost set. Run knife around rim of pan to loosen cake; cool before removing rim. Refrigerate 4 hours.

Nutrition Information

- Calories: 410
- Protein: 8 g
- Total Fat: 28 g
- Cholesterol: 145 mg
- Sugar: 0 g
- Total Carbohydrate: 0 g
- Fiber: 0 g
- Sodium: 340 mg
- Saturated Fat: 16 g

39. Easy Caramel Pecan Cheesecake

Serving: 0 | Prep: 15mins | Cook: 1hours | Ready in: 1hours15mins

Ingredients

- 2 pkg. (11.1 oz. each) JELL-O No Bake Real Cheesecake Dessert
- 1/4 cup sugar
- 10 Tbsp. margarine or butter, melted
- 2 Tbsp. water
- 2 cups chopped toasted PLANTERS Pecans, divided
- 1-1/2 cups caramel ice cream topping, divided
- 3 cups cold milk

Direction

- Mix Crust Mixes, sugar, margarine and water in large bowl until well blended. Firmly press half of the crumb mixture 1-1/2 inches up side of 9-inch springform pan. Press remaining crumb mixture firmly onto bottom of pan, using bottom of a dry measuring cup. Sprinkle 1 cup of the pecans onto bottom of crust. Drizzle with 3/4 cup of the caramel topping.
- Pour milk into large bowl. Add Filling Mixes. Beat with electric mixer on low speed just until blended. Beat on medium speed 3 minutes. (Filling will be thick.) Spoon into crust.
- Refrigerate at least 1 hour or until firm. Run knife or metal spatula around rim of pan to loosen cake; remove rim of pan. Sprinkle with remaining 1 cup pecans and drizzle with remaining 3/4 cup caramel topping just before serving. Store leftover cheesecake in refrigerator.

Nutrition Information

- Calories: 450
- Total Fat: 22 g
- Sugar: 38 g
- Saturated Fat: 4.5 g
- Sodium: 460 mg
- Protein: 6 g
- Total Carbohydrate: 59 g
- Cholesterol: 5 mg
- Fiber: 2 g

40. Easy Mini Cheesecakes

Serving: 12 | Prep: 10mins | Cook: 3hours20mins | Ready in: 3hours30mins

Ingredients

- 2 pkg. (8 oz. each) PHILADELPHIA Cream Cheese, softened
- 1/2 cup sugar
- 1/2 tsp. vanilla
- 2 eggs
- 15 chocolate chip cookies (2 inch), divided
- 12 fresh strawberries, quartered

Direction

- Heat oven to 350°F.
- Beat cream cheese, sugar and vanilla in large bowl with mixer until blended. Add eggs, 1 at a time, mixing on low speed after each just until blended.
- Place 1 cookie in bottom of each of 12 (2-1/2-inch) foil baking cups. Place in muffin cups; fill evenly with batter. Cut remaining cookies into quarters; set aside for later use.
- Bake 20 min. or until centers are almost set. Cool completely. Refrigerate 3 hours or until chilled. Top with cookie pieces and strawberries just before serving.

Nutrition Information

- Calories: 240
- Fiber: 1 g
- Cholesterol: 80 mg
- Total Fat: 17 g
- Protein: 4 g
- Saturated Fat: 9 g
- Sugar: 0 g
- Sodium: 200 mg
- Total Carbohydrate: 0 g

41. Eggnog Cheesecake Recipe

Serving: 16 | Prep: 25mins | Cook: 6hours15mins | Ready in: 6hours40mins

Ingredients

- 8 soft oatmeal cookies (2 inch), crumbled (about 1-1/2 cups)
- 4 pkg. (8 oz. each) PHILADELPHIA Cream Cheese, softened
- 1 cup sugar
- 1 tsp. ground nutmeg
- 1 tsp. vanilla
- 2 Tbsp. rum
- 4 eggs
- 1/2 cup whipping cream

Direction

- Heat oven to 325°F.
- Press cookie crumbs onto bottom of 9-inch springform pan.
- Beat cream cheese, sugar, nutmeg, vanilla and 2 Tbsp. rum with mixer until blended. Add eggs 1 at a time, mixing on low speed after each just until blended; pour over crust.
- Bake 1 hour 10 min. to 1 hour 15 min. or until center is almost set. Run knife around rim of pan to loosen cake; cool before removing rim. Refrigerate cheesecake 4 hours.
- Beat cream in small bowl with mixer on high speed until stiff peaks form. Spread over cheesecake.

Nutrition Information

- Calories: 320
- Total Fat: 24 g
- Saturated Fat: 14 g
- Sodium: 260 mg
- Cholesterol: 130 mg
- Fiber: 0 g
- Protein: 6 g
- Sugar: 0 g
- Total Carbohydrate: 0 g

42. English Toffee Cheesecake

Serving: 0 | Prep: 30mins | Cook: 4hours35mins | Ready in: 5hours5mins

Ingredients

- 1 cup graham cracker crumbs
- 2 Tbsp. granulated sugar
- 3 Tbsp. butter or margarine, melted
- 3 pkg. (8 oz. each) PHILADELPHIA Cream Cheese, softened
- 3/4 cup firmly packed dark brown sugar
- 2 tsp. vanilla
- 3 eggs
- 4 chocolate-covered toffee bars (1.4 oz. each), coarsely chopped, divided

Direction

- Preheat oven to 350°F if using a silver 9-inch springform pan (or 325°F if using a dark nonstick 9-inch springform pan). Mix crumbs, granulated sugar and butter; press firmly onto bottom of pan. Bake 10 min.; cool. Increase oven temperature to 450°F.
- Beat cream cheese and brown sugar in large bowl with electric mixer on medium speed until well blended. Add vanilla; mix well. Add eggs, 1 at a time, mixing on low speed after each addition just until blended. Stir in 1/2 cup of the candy. Pour over crust.
- Bake 10 min. Reduce oven temperature to 250°F; continue baking 25 min. or until center is almost set. Run small knife or metal spatula around rim of pan to loosen cake; cool before removing rim of pan. Refrigerate several hours or overnight. Top with remaining candy just before serving. Store leftover cheesecake in refrigerator.

Nutrition Information

- Calories: 380
- Total Fat: 26 g
- Saturated Fat: 16 g
- Total Carbohydrate: 0 g
- Sugar: 0 g
- Protein: 6 g
- Fiber: 0.6282 g
- Cholesterol: 135 mg
- Sodium: 370 mg

43. Festive Irish Cream Cheesecake

Serving: 10 | Prep: 25mins | Cook: 4hours | Ready in: 4hours25mins

Ingredients

- 1 cup graham cracker crumbs
- 1-1/4 cups sugar, divided
- 1/4 cup butter or margarine, melted
- 1 env. KNOX Unflavored Gelatine
- 1/2 cup cold water, divided
- 2 pkg. (8 oz. each) PHILADELPHIA Cream Cheese, softened
- 2 Tbsp. unsweetened cocoa powder
- 2 Tbsp. Irish cream liqueur
- 1 tub (8 oz.) COOL WHIP Whipped Topping, thawed
- 2 oz. BAKER'S Semi-Sweet Chocolate

Direction

- Mix crumbs, 1/4 cup sugar and butter; press onto bottom of 9-inch springform pan.
- Sprinkle gelatine over 1/4 cup water in small saucepan; let stand 1 min. Cook and stir on low heat 3 min. or until gelatine is completely dissolved.
- Beat cream cheese, remaining sugar and cocoa in large bowl with mixer until blended. Gradually beat in gelatine mixture, then remaining water and liqueur; refrigerate until slightly thickened. Gently stir in COOL WHIP; pour over crust. Refrigerate several hours or until firm. Meanwhile, melt chocolate as directed on package; use to make chocolate curls. (See Tip.)
- Top cheesecake with chocolate curls just before serving.

Nutrition Information

- Calories: 470
- Fiber: 0.7718 g

- Total Carbohydrate: 45 g
- Cholesterol: 65 mg
- Total Fat: 28 g
- Protein: 5 g
- Sugar: 36 g
- Saturated Fat: 18 g
- Sodium: 260 mg

44. Frozen Lemon Blueberry Cheesecake

Serving: 16 | Prep: 20mins | Cook: 6hours | Ready in: 6hours20mins

Ingredients

- 24 gingersnaps, finely crushed (about 1-1/4 cups)
- 1/4 cup butter, melted
- 2 pkg. (8 oz. each) PHILADELPHIA Cream Cheese, softened
- 1 can (14 oz.) sweetened condensed milk
- 1 Tbsp. zest and 1/4 cup juice from 2 lemons
- 1 cup thawed COOL WHIP Whipped Topping
- 2 cups blueberries
- 1/4 cup sugar
- 2 Tbsp. water
- 1/4 tsp. ground ginger

Direction

- Combine gingersnap crumbs and butter; press onto bottom of 9-inch springform pan.
- Beat cream cheese in large bowl with mixer until creamy. Gradually beat in milk. Blend in lemon zest and juice. Whisk in COOL WHIP; spoon over crust.
- Freeze 6 hours or until firm. Meanwhile, cook remaining ingredients in saucepan on medium heat 4 min., stirring occasionally; cool. Refrigerate until ready to serve.
- Let cheesecake stand at room temperature 15 min. before serving topped with blueberry sauce.

Nutrition Information

- Calories: 270
- Sodium: 240 mg
- Protein: 4 g
- Sugar: 0 g
- Total Carbohydrate: 0 g
- Fiber: 0.5609 g
- Cholesterol: 50 mg
- Total Fat: 15 g
- Saturated Fat: 10 g

45. Frozen Mini Cinnamon Coffee Cheesecakes

Serving: 0 | Prep: 15mins | Cook: 3hours | Ready in: 3hours15mins

Ingredients

- 12 gingersnaps, divided
- 2 Tbsp. MAXWELL HOUSE Naturally Decaffeinated Instant Coffee
- 1 Tbsp. water
- 1/2 cup granular no-calorie sweetener
- 1 tub (8 oz.) PHILADELPHIA 1/3 Less Fat than Cream Cheese
- 1 tsp. vanilla
- 1/4 tsp. ground cinnamon
- 1-1/2 cups thawed COOL WHIP LITE Whipped Topping
- 1 cup fresh raspberries

Direction

- Place 1 cookie each of 12 paper-lined muffin cups.
- Dissolve coffee granules in water in large bowl. Add granulated sweetener, reduced-fat cream cheese, vanilla and cinnamon; beat with whisk until well blended. Stir in COOL WHIP; spoon into muffin cups. Top with berries.
- Freeze 3 hours or until firm. Remove cheesecakes from freezer 10 min. before

serving. Let stand at room temperature to soften slightly.

Nutrition Information

- Calories: 100
- Protein: 2 g
- Sodium: 125 mg
- Total Fat: 5 g
- Cholesterol: 10 mg
- Sugar: 0 g
- Total Carbohydrate: 0 g
- Fiber: 0.7094 g
- Saturated Fat: 3.5 g

46. JELL O® Eggnog Cheesecake

Serving: 16 | Prep: 30mins | Cook: 3hours | Ready in: 3hours30mins

Ingredients

- 2 pkg. (5-1/2 oz. each) chocolate-laced pirouette cookies
- 1/3 cup graham cracker crumbs
- 3 Tbsp. butter or margarine, melted
- 2 pkg. (8 oz. each) PHILADELPHIA Cream Cheese, softened
- 2 cups eggnog, divided
- 1 cup milk
- 2 pkg. (4-serving size each) JELL-O French Vanilla Flavor Instant Pudding
- 1 Tbsp. light rum
- 1/8 tsp. ground nutmeg

Direction

- Cut 1-inch piece off one end of each cookie; crush into fine crumbs. Place in medium bowl. Set aside remaining cookie pieces for later use. Add graham crumbs and butter to cookie crumbs; mix well. Press firmly onto bottom of 9-inch springform pan; set aside.

- Beat cream cheese in large bowl with electric mixer on medium speed until creamy. Gradually add 1 cup of the eggnog, mixing until well blended. Add remaining 1 cup eggnog, the milk, dry pudding mixes, rum and nutmeg; beat 1 min. or until well blended. Pour over crust.
- Refrigerate 3 hours or until firm. Run knife or metal spatula around rim of pan to loosen cake; remove rim of pan. Press reserved cookie pieces into side of cheesecake. Store leftover cheesecake in refrigerator.

Nutrition Information

- Calories: 320
- Total Fat: 18 g
- Saturated Fat: 10 g
- Total Carbohydrate: 30 g
- Sugar: 25 g
- Sodium: 370 mg
- Cholesterol: 55 mg
- Fiber: 1 g
- Protein: 4 g

47. JELL O® No Bake Pineapple Cheesecake Bars

Serving: 0 | Prep: 10mins | Cook: 1hours | Ready in: 1hours10mins

Ingredients

- 1 pkg. (11.1 oz.) JELL-O No Bake Real Cheesecake Dessert
- 2 Tbsp. sugar
- 5 Tbsp. margarine, melted
- 1 Tbsp. water
- 1 tsp. ground ginger
- 1 can (20 oz.) crushed pineapple, well drained, divided
- 1-1/2 cups cold milk
- 2 tsp. grated lemon zest

Direction

- Mix Crust Mix, sugar, margarine, water and ginger with fork in 9-inch square pan until well blended. Reserve 2 Tbsp. of the crumb mixture. Press remaining crumb mixture firmly onto bottom of pan with dry measuring cup; cover with half of the pineapple.
- Beat milk, Filling Mix and lemon zest with electric mixer on low speed just until blended. Beat on medium speed 3 minutes. (Filling will be thick.) Spoon over pineapple layer in crust.
- Refrigerate at least 1 hour. Top with remaining pineapple and reserved 2 Tbsp. crumb mixture. Serve immediately or cover and refrigerate until ready to serve. Cut into 8 bars. Store leftover bars in refrigerator.

Nutrition Information

- Calories: 290
- Total Carbohydrate: 43 g
- Fiber: 1 g
- Saturated Fat: 4 g
- Protein: 4 g
- Cholesterol: 5 mg
- Total Fat: 12 g
- Sodium: 390 mg
- Sugar: 30 g

48. Key Lime Mini Cheesecakes

Serving: 12 | Prep: 20mins | Cook: 3hours | Ready in: 3hours20mins

Ingredients

- 1 cup graham cracker crumbs
- 3/4 cup plus 3 Tbsp. sugar, divided
- 3 Tbsp. butter or margarine, melted
- 3 pkg. (8 oz. each) PHILADELPHIA Cream Cheese, softened
- 1 Tbsp. flour
- 1 tsp. key lime zest

- 1 Tbsp. key lime juice
- 3 eggs

Direction

- Heat oven to 325°F.
- Mix graham crumbs, 3 Tbsp. sugar and butter until blended; press onto bottoms of 12 paper-lined muffin cups.
- Beat cream cheese, remaining sugar, flour, lime zest and juice with mixer until blended. Add eggs, 1 at a time, mixing on low speed after each just until blended. Spoon over crusts.
- Bake 25 to 30 min. or until centers are almost set. Cool completely. Refrigerate 2 hours.

Nutrition Information

- Calories: 330
- Protein: 6 g
- Sugar: 0 g
- Total Fat: 23 g
- Cholesterol: 130 mg
- Fiber: 0 g
- Total Carbohydrate: 0 g
- Sodium: 300 mg
- Saturated Fat: 14 g

49. Layered Coconut Cream Cheesecake Bars

Serving: 16 | Prep: 20mins | Cook: 5hours | Ready in: 5hours20mins

Ingredients

- 84 vanilla wafers, divided
- 6 Tbsp. butter, melted
- 1 pkg. (8 oz.) PHILADELPHIA Cream Cheese, softened
- 2 Tbsp. sugar
- 1 tub (8 oz.) COOL WHIP Whipped Topping, thawed, divided

- 2 pkg. (3.4 oz. each) JELL-O Vanilla Flavor Instant Pudding
- 2-1/2 cups cold milk
- 1-1/2 cups BAKER'S ANGEL FLAKE Coconut, toasted, divided

Direction

- Reserve 24 wafers. Crush remaining wafers; mix with butter. Press onto bottom of 13x9-inch pan. Refrigerate until ready to use.
- Beat cream cheese and sugar with mixer until blended. Whisk in 1 cup COOL WHIP; spread carefully over crust. Stand reserved wafers around edges.
- Beat pudding mixes and milk in medium bowl with whisk 2 min. Stir in 1 cup of the remaining COOL WHIP and 3/4 cup coconut; spread over cream cheese layer. Top with remaining COOL WHIP and coconut. Refrigerate 5 hours.

Nutrition Information

- Calories: 340
- Cholesterol: 35 mg
- Sugar: 0 g
- Total Carbohydrate: 0 g
- Saturated Fat: 13 g
- Total Fat: 20 g
- Sodium: 380 mg
- Fiber: 0.8186 g
- Protein: 3 g

50. Lemon Meringue Cheesecake

Serving: 16 | Prep: 25mins | Cook: 6hours20mins | Ready in: 6hours45mins

Ingredients

- 1-1/2 cups graham cracker crumbs
- 1/4 cup butter, melted
- 1-3/4 cups sugar, divided
- 3 lemons
- 4 eggs, divided
- 4 pkg. (8 oz. each) PHILADELPHIA Cream Cheese, softened
- 1 cup BREAKSTONE'S or KNUDSEN Sour Cream
- 1/4 tsp. cream of tartar

Direction

- Heat oven to 325°F.
- Mix crumbs, butter and 2 Tbsp. sugar; press onto bottom of 9-inch springform pan. Grate zest from 1 lemon, then squeeze 1/2 cup juice from all lemons. Separate 3 eggs.
- Beat cream cheese and 1 cup of the remaining sugar in large bowl with mixer until blended. Add sour cream and lemon juice; mix well. Add 1 whole egg and 3 yolks, 1 at a time, mixing on low speed after each just until blended. Stir in zest. Pour over crust.
- Bake 1 hour 10 min. or until center is set; remove from oven. Increase oven temperature to 400°F.
- Beat egg whites and cream of tartar in small bowl with mixer on high speed until foamy. Gradually add remaining sugar, beating until stiff peaks form; spoon onto cheesecake. Spread to completely cover top. Bake 8 to 10 min. or until golden brown. Run knife around rim of pan to loosen cake; cool before removing rim. Refrigerate 4 hours.

Nutrition Information

- Calories: 400
- Total Fat: 27 g
- Cholesterol: 125 mg
- Total Carbohydrate: 0 g
- Sodium: 310 mg
- Fiber: 0.556 g
- Sugar: 0 g
- Protein: 6 g
- Saturated Fat: 16 g

51. Lemon Refrigerator Cheesecake

Serving: 0 | Prep: 30mins | Cook: 3hours | Ready in: 3hours30mins

Ingredients

- 1-1/2 cups graham cracker crumbs
- 1/2 cup (1 stick) butter or margarine, melted
- 3/4 cup sugar, divided
- 1 tsp. ground cinnamon
- 1 env. KNOX Unflavored Gelatine
- 3/4 cup cold water, divided
- 2 pkg. (8 oz. each) PHILADELPHIA Cream Cheese, softened
- 1 Tbsp. grated lemon zest
- 3 Tbsp. lemon juice
- 1 cup whipping cream, whipped

Direction

- Mix graham crumbs, butter, 1/4 cup of the sugar and the cinnamon until well blended. Remove 1/2 cup of the crumb mixture; set aside for later use. Press remaining crumb mixture firmly onto bottom of 9-inch springform pan. Sprinkle dry gelatine over 1/4 cup of the water in small saucepan. Let stand 1 minute. Cook on low heat 5 minutes or until gelatine is completely dissolved, stirring occasionally.
- Beat cream cheese and remaining 1/2 cup sugar in large bowl with electric mixer on medium speed until well blended. Gradually add gelatine mixture, remaining 1/2 cup water, the lemon peel and juice. Refrigerate until slightly thickened. Gently stir in whipped cream; pour over crust. Sprinkle with the reserved crumb mixture.
- Refrigerate several hours or until firm. Run small knife or metal spatula around rim of pan to loosen cake; remove rim of pan. Store leftover cheesecake in refrigerator.

Nutrition Information

- Calories: 370
- Fiber: 1 g
- Total Fat: 29 g
- Total Carbohydrate: 25 g
- Cholesterol: 90 mg
- Sugar: 17 g
- Sodium: 290 mg
- Protein: 4 g
- Saturated Fat: 17 g

52. Lemon Blueberry Cheesecake Jars

Serving: 8 | Prep: 20mins | Cook: 2hours30mins | Ready in: 2hours50mins

Ingredients

- 1-1/2 cups blueberries
- 2 tsp. flour
- Zest and 1 Tbsp. juice from 1 lemon, divided
- 1/2 cup honey, divided
- 1 pkg. (8 oz.) PHILADELPHIA Cream Cheese, softened
- 2/3 cup plain low-fat Greek-style yogurt
- 1/2 tsp. vanilla
- 1/4 cup graham cracker crumbs
- 1/4 cup PLANTERS Sliced Almonds, ground
- 1 Tbsp. butter, melted

Direction

- Combine blueberries, flour, lemon juice and 1/4 cup honey in medium saucepan. Cook on medium heat 5 to 8 min. or until blueberries are softened and sauce is thickened, stirring frequently. Cool.
- Beat cream cheese, yogurt, vanilla, lemon zest and remaining honey in medium bowl with mixer until blended.
- Combine graham crumbs, nuts and butter; spoon into 8 (4-oz.) jars, adding about 1 Tbsp. crumb mixture to each jar. Top with layers of cream cheese mixture and blueberry sauce.
- Refrigerate 2 hours.

Nutrition Information

- Calories: 240
- Saturated Fat: 7 g
- Cholesterol: 35 mg
- Total Carbohydrate: 0 g
- Sugar: 0 g
- Protein: 5 g
- Total Fat: 13 g
- Sodium: 140 mg
- Fiber: 1 g

53. Lemon White Chocolate Mini Cheesecakes

Serving: 12 | Prep: 15mins | Cook: 3hours5mins | Ready in: 3hours20mins

Ingredients

- 1 pkg. (4 oz.) BAKER'S White Chocolate, divided
- 28 square shortbread cookies (1-1/2 inch), divided
- 2 Tbsp. butter, melted
- 1/2 cup plus 2 Tbsp. sugar, divided
- 2 pkg. (8 oz. each) PHILADELPHIA Cream Cheese, softened
- 1 tsp. vanilla
- 1 tsp. zest and 1/4 cup juice from 2 lemons
- 2 eggs

Direction

- Heat oven to 325°F.
- Melt 2 oz. chocolate as directed on package; set aside for later use.
- Use pulsing action of food processor to process 16 cookies until finely crushed; spoon into medium bowl. Add butter and 2 Tbsp. sugar; mix well. Press onto bottoms of 12 paper-lined muffin cups, adding about 1 Tbsp. crumb mixture to each prepared cup.
- Beat cream cheese, vanilla and remaining sugar in large bowl with mixer until blended.

Add lemon zest, lemon juice and melted chocolate; mix well. Add eggs, 1 at a time, mixing on low speed after each just until blended. Spoon over crusts.
- Bake 17 to 20 min. or until centers are almost set. Cool completely.
- Melt remaining chocolate. Coarsely chop remaining cookies; sprinkle over cheesecakes. Drizzle with melted chocolate.
- Refrigerate 2 hours.

Nutrition Information

- Calories: 330
- Cholesterol: 80 mg
- Saturated Fat: 12 g
- Sodium: 260 mg
- Total Carbohydrate: 27 g
- Fiber: 0 g
- Sugar: 18 g
- Total Fat: 23 g
- Protein: 5 g

54. Low Fat Orange Dream Cheesecake

Serving: 0 | Prep: 15mins | Cook: 4hours | Ready in: 4hours15mins

Ingredients

- 1 graham cracker, crushed
- 2/3 cup boiling water
- 1 pkg. (.3 oz.) JELL-O Orange Flavor Sugar Free Gelatin
- 1 cup BREAKSTONE'S or KNUDSEN 2% Milkfat Low Fat Cottage Cheese
- 1 tub (8 oz.) PHILADELPHIA 1/3 Less Fat than Cream Cheese
- 2 cups thawed COOL WHIP FREE Whipped Topping

Direction

- Sprinkle crumbs onto bottom of 8- or 9-inch springform pan sprayed with cooking spray.
- Add boiling water to gelatin mix; stir 2 min. until completely dissolved. Cool 5 min.; pour into blender. Add cottage cheese and cream cheese; blend well. Pour into large bowl. Whisk in COOL WHIP. Pour into prepared pan; smooth top.
- Refrigerate 4 hours or until firm. When ready to serve, run knife around rim of pan to loosen cake; remove rim.

Nutrition Information

- Calories: 170
- Protein: 9 g
- Fiber: 0 g
- Saturated Fat: 3.5 g
- Sodium: 490 mg
- Cholesterol: 20 mg
- Sugar: 0 g
- Total Fat: 5 g
- Total Carbohydrate: 0 g

55. Marbled Chocolate Cheesecake

Serving: 0 | Prep: 10mins | Cook: 4hours10mins | Ready in: 4hours20mins

Ingredients

- 1 pkg. (4 oz.) BAKER'S Semi-Sweet Chocolate
- 2 pkg. (8 oz. each) PHILADELPHIA Cream Cheese, softened, divided
- 1/2 cup sugar, divided
- 2 eggs, divided
- 1 OREO Pie Crust (6 oz.)
- 1/2 tsp. vanilla

Direction

- Heat oven to 350°F.

- Microwave chocolate in large microwaveable bowl on HIGH 1-1/2 min., stirring every 30 sec. Stir until chocolate is completely melted.
- Add 1 pkg. cream cheese, 1/4 cup sugar and 1 egg; beat with whisk until well blended. Pour into crust.
- Beat remaining cream cheese, sugar, egg and vanilla in same bowl with whisk until well blended. Spoon over chocolate batter; swirl gently with knife.
- Bake 40 min. or until center is almost set. Cool. Refrigerate 3 hours. Let stand at room temperature 10 min. before serving.

Nutrition Information

- Calories: 430
- Fiber: 2 g
- Protein: 7 g
- Total Fat: 31 g
- Saturated Fat: 16 g
- Sodium: 370 mg
- Total Carbohydrate: 37 g
- Cholesterol: 110 mg
- Sugar: 28 g

56. Marshmallow Cookie Cheesecake

Serving: 0 | Prep: 15mins | Cook: 6hours | Ready in: 6hours15mins

Ingredients

- 1-3/4 cups graham cracker crumbs
- 1 cup sugar, divided
- 1/3 cup margarine or butter, melted
- 3 pkg. (8 oz. each) PHILADELPHIA Cream Cheese, softened
- 1 cup BREAKSTONE'S or KNUDSEN Sour Cream
- 1 tsp. vanilla
- 4 eggs
- 15 chocolate-covered marshmallow cookies

Direction

- Preheat oven to 350°F if using a silver 9-inch springform pan (or to 325°F if using a dark nonstick 9-inch springform pan). Mix graham cracker crumbs, 1/4 cup of the sugar and the margarine. Press firmly onto bottom and 2 inches up side of pan; set aside.
- Beat cream cheese and remaining 3/4 cup sugar in small bowl with electric mixer on medium speed until well blended. Add sour cream and vanilla; mix well. Add eggs, 1 at a time, mixing just until blended after each addition. Arrange cakes on crust; cover with batter.
- Bake 1 hour or until center is almost set. Turn oven off; open door slightly. Let cheesecake stand in oven 1 hour. Remove from oven; cool on wire rack at room temperature. Refrigerate at least 4 hours or until chilled. Store leftover cheesecake in refrigerator.

Nutrition Information

- Calories: 380
- Sodium: 320 mg
- Sugar: 0 g
- Total Carbohydrate: 0 g
- Total Fat: 26 g
- Protein: 6 g
- Saturated Fat: 14 g
- Cholesterol: 110 mg
- Fiber: 1 g

57. Mini Classic Cheesecake Recipe

Serving: 12 | Prep: 15mins | Cook: 4hours20mins | Ready in: 4hours35mins

Ingredients

- 1 cup graham cracker crumbs
- 3 Tbsp. butter, melted

- 2 pkg. (8 oz. each) PHILADELPHIA Cream Cheese, softened
- 1/2 cup sugar
- 1 tsp. vanilla
- 2 eggs

Direction

- Heat oven to 350°F.
- Mix graham crumbs and butter; press evenly onto bottoms of 12 muffin cups sprayed with cooking spray.
- Beat cream cheese, sugar and vanilla in large bowl with mixer until blended. Add eggs, 1 at a time, mixing on low speed after each just until blended. Pour evenly over crusts.
- Bake 20 min. or until center is almost set. Cool completely. Refrigerate 3 hours.

Nutrition Information

- Calories: 240
- Total Fat: 17 g
- Protein: 4 g
- Sodium: 220 mg
- Total Carbohydrate: 16 g
- Sugar: 12 g
- Saturated Fat: 10 g
- Cholesterol: 80 mg
- Fiber: 0 g

58. Mini Coconut Cheesecakes Bites

Serving: 24 | Prep: 15mins | Cook: 1hours44mins | Ready in: 1hours59mins

Ingredients

- 1 pkg. (16.5 oz.) refrigerated sugar cookie dough
- 1 pkg. (8 oz.) PHILADELPHIA Cream Cheese, softened
- 1/4 cup butter, softened

- 1/4 cup sugar
- 1 tsp. vanilla
- 1-1/2 cups thawed COOL WHIP Whipped Topping
- 1-1/4 cups BAKER'S ANGEL FLAKE Coconut, toasted, divided

Direction

- Heat oven to 350°F.
- Roll cookie dough into 24 (1-inch) balls; place 1 ball in each of 24 mini muffin pan cups sprayed with cooking spray.
- Bake 11 to 14 min. or until lightly browned. Immediately use handle of wooden spoon to make shallow indentation in center of each cookie cup. Cool 10 min. Run knife around edges of cups to loosen from sides of pan. Remove from pan to wire racks; cool completely.
- Beat cream cheese and butter in medium bowl with mixer until blended. Add sugar and vanilla; mix well. Gently stir in COOL WHIP and 1 cup coconut.
- Spoon cream cheese mixture into resealable plastic bag. Cut small piece off one bottom corner of bag; use to pipe cream cheese mixture into cookie cups. Top with remaining coconut.
- Refrigerate 1 hour.

Nutrition Information

- Calories: 180
- Total Carbohydrate: 18 g
- Saturated Fat: 7 g
- Sodium: 130 mg
- Cholesterol: 25 mg
- Fiber: 0 g
- Sugar: 12 g
- Protein: 2 g
- Total Fat: 12 g

59. Mini Lemon Cheesecakes

Serving: 6 | Prep: 20mins | Cook: 2hours40mins | Ready in: 3hours

Ingredients

- 40 vanilla wafers, finely crushed (about 1-2/3 cups)
- zest and 1 Tbsp. juice from 1 lemon, divided
- 1/4 cup butter or margarine, softened
- 1 pkg. (8 oz.) PHILADELPHIA Cream Cheese, softened
- 1/2 cup sugar
- 1 egg

Direction

- Heat oven to 350°F.
- Mix wafer crumbs, butter and 2 tsp. lemon zest until blended. Spoon about 2 Tbsp. crumb mixture into each of 12 paper-lined muffin cups. Press crumb mixture onto bottoms and up sides of prepared cups.
- Beat cream cheese with mixer until creamy. Gradually add sugar, beating after each addition until well blended. Add egg, lemon juice and remaining zest; beat just until blended. Spoon into crusts.
- Bake 40 min. or until lightly browned. Turn oven off. Let cheesecakes stand in oven 20 min., leaving door slightly ajar. Remove to wire rack; cool completely.
- Refrigerate 1 hour. Remove from paper liners before serving.

Nutrition Information

- Calories: 390
- Sugar: 26 g
- Total Fat: 26 g
- Sodium: 310 mg
- Fiber: 0 g
- Cholesterol: 105 mg
- Protein: 5 g
- Saturated Fat: 14 g
- Total Carbohydrate: 36 g

60. Mini Pumpkin Spice Latte Cheesecakes

Serving: 24 | Prep: 30mins | Cook: 3hours30mins | Ready in: 4hours

Ingredients

- 24 European-style cookies for coffee (speculoos cookies), finely crushed (about 1-3/4 cups)
- 1 cup sugar, divided
- 3 pkg. (8 oz. each) PHILADELPHIA Cream Cheese, softened
- 3/4 cup canned pumpkin
- 2-1/4 tsp. pumpkin pie spice, divided
- 1 tsp. vanilla
- 3 eggs
- 1 Tbsp. MAXWELL HOUSE Instant Coffee
- 1 cup whipping cream

Direction

- Heat oven to 325°F.
- Combine cookie crumbs and 2 Tbsp. sugar; press onto bottoms of 24 paper-lined muffin cups, adding about 1 Tbsp. crumb mixture to each cup.
- Beat cream cheese and 3/4 cup of the remaining sugar in large bowl with mixer until blended. Add pumpkin, 2 tsp. pumpkin pie spice and vanilla; mix well. Add eggs, 1 at a time, mixing on low speed after each just until blended. Stir in coffee granules until completely dissolved. Spoon over crusts.
- Bake 26 to 30 min. or until centers are almost set. Cool completely. Refrigerate 2 hours.
- Beat whipping cream with remaining 2 Tbsp. sugar in clean bowl with mixer on high speed until stiff peaks form. Spoon into pastry bag; use to pipe whipped cream over cheesecakes. Sprinkle with remaining pumpkin pie spice.

Nutrition Information

- Calories: 210
- Protein: 3 g
- Sugar: 0 g
- Total Fat: 15 g
- Cholesterol: 75 mg
- Fiber: 0 g
- Sodium: 150 mg
- Total Carbohydrate: 0 g
- Saturated Fat: 9 g

61. Mini Strawberry Cheesecakes

Serving: 0 | Prep: 15mins | Cook: 1hours | Ready in: 1hours15mins

Ingredients

- 1 pkg. (8 oz.) PHILADELPHIA Neufchatel Cheese, softened
- 1 pkg. (3.4 oz.) JELL-O Strawberry Crème Flavor Instant Pudding
- 1 cup cold fat-free milk
- 2 cups thawed COOL WHIP LITE Whipped Topping
- 24 vanilla wafers
- 1 cup sliced fresh strawberries

Direction

- Beat Neufchatel with mixer until creamy. Blend in dry pudding mix. Gradually beat in milk. Stir in COOL WHIP.
- Place 1 wafer in each of 24 paper-lined muffin cups; cover with pudding mixture.
- Freeze 1 hour. Top with berries just before serving.

Nutrition Information

- Calories: 80
- Sodium: 120 mg
- Fiber: 0 g
- Protein: 1 g

- Total Carbohydrate: 0 g
- Total Fat: 4 g
- Cholesterol: 10 mg
- Sugar: 0 g
- Saturated Fat: 3 g

62. Mocha Cheesecake Minis

Serving: 12 | Prep: 30mins | Cook: 1hours5mins |Ready in: 1hours35mins

Ingredients

- 10 vanilla creme-filled chocolate sandwich cookies, finely crushed (about 3/4 cup)
- 2 Tbsp. butter, melted
- 2 pkg. (8 oz. each) PHILADELPHIA Cream Cheese, softened
- 1/2 cup sugar
- 2 eggs
- 1 tsp. MAXWELL HOUSE Instant Coffee
- 2 tsp. water
- 1 pkg. (4 oz.) BAKER'S Semi-Sweet Chocolate, melted, cooled
- 1-1/8 tsp. unsweetened cocoa powder, divided
- 1 cup thawed COOL WHIP Whipped Topping
- 24 chocolate-covered coffee beans

Direction

- Heat oven to 350°F.
- Mix cookie crumbs and butter; press about 1 Tbsp. onto bottom of each of 12 foil-lined muffin cups. Bake 8 min.
- Beat cream cheese and sugar with mixer until blended. Add eggs; beat just until blended. Dissolve coffee in water. Add to batter with melted chocolate; beat until blended. Spoon about 1/4 cup batter into each cup. (Cups will be full.)
- Bake 23 to 25 min. or until centers are almost set. Cool completely.
- Add 1 tsp. cocoa powder to COOL WHIP; stir gently until blended. Spoon into pastry bag

fitted with decorating tip; use to pipe COOL WHIP mixture onto cheesecakes. Garnish with remaining cocoa powder and coffee beans.

Nutrition Information

- Calories: 340
- Total Fat: 24 g
- Total Carbohydrate: 28 g
- Saturated Fat: 14 g
- Cholesterol: 90 mg
- Sodium: 220 mg
- Fiber: 2 g
- Sugar: 22 g
- Protein: 5 g

63. New York Style Mini Cheesecake Bites

Serving: 24 | Prep: 15mins | Cook: 3hours15mins |Ready in: 3hours30mins

Ingredients

- 24 mini chocolate chip cookies
- 1 pkg. (8 oz.) PHILADELPHIA Cream Cheese, softened
- 1/4 cup sugar
- 1 tsp. vanilla
- 1/4 cup BREAKSTONE'S or KNUDSEN Sour Cream
- 1 Tbsp. flour
- 1 egg
- 3/4 cup cherry pie filling

Direction

- Heat oven to 350°F.
- Place 1 cookie, flat side down, in each of 24 paper-lined mini muffin pan cups. Beat cream cheese, sugar and vanilla with mixer until blended. Add sour cream and flour; mix well. Add egg; beat on low speed just until blended. Spoon over cookies.

- Bake 13 to 15 min. or until centers are almost set.
- Cool 1 hour before removing from pan. Refrigerate 2 hours.
- Top with pie filling just before serving.

Nutrition Information

- Calories: 90
- Total Fat: 5 g
- Cholesterol: 20 mg
- Sodium: 55 mg
- Saturated Fat: 3 g
- Fiber: 0 g
- Protein: 1 g
- Sugar: 4 g
- Total Carbohydrate: 10 g

64. No Bake Cheesecake Bars

Serving: 0 | Prep: | Cook: | Ready in:

Ingredients

- 1-1/2 cups graham cracker crumbs
- 1/4 cup butter, melted
- 2 Tbsp. sugar
- 2 pkg. (4 oz. each) BAKER'S Semi-Sweet Chocolate, divided
- 4 pkg. (8 oz. each) PHILADELPHIA Cream Cheese, softened
- 1/2 cup sugar
- 1 tsp. vanilla
- 1 tub (8 oz.) COOL WHIP Whipped Topping, thawed

Direction

- Line 13x9-inch pan with foil, with ends of foil extending over sides. Mix graham crumbs, butter and 2 Tbsp. sugar; press onto bottom of pan. Refrigerate while preparing filling.
- Melt 6 oz. chocolate as directed on package; cool slightly. Beat cream cheese, 1/2 cup sugar

and vanilla in large bowl with mixer until blended. Gently stir in COOL WHIP. Pour half the batter into medium bowl; stir in melted chocolate. Pour over crust; cover with remaining plain batter. Melt remaining chocolate; drizzle over batter.
- Refrigerate 3 hours or until firm. Use foil handles to remove cheesecake from pan before cutting to serve.

Nutrition Information

- Calories: 0 g
- Total Carbohydrate: 0 g
- Total Fat: 0 g
- Sugar: 0 g
- Cholesterol: 0 g
- Fiber: 0 g
- Sodium: 0 g
- Protein: 0 g
- Saturated Fat: 0 g

65. No Bake OREO Cheesecake Recipe

Serving: 0 | Prep: 10mins | Cook: | Ready in: 10mins

Ingredients

- 1 tub (24.2 oz.) PHILADELPHIA Ready-To-Eat Cheesecake Filling
- 12 OREO Cookies, coarsely chopped, divided
- 1 OREO Pie Crust (6 oz.)

Direction

- Spoon cheesecake filling into large bowl. Remove 1/3 cup of the chopped cookies; set aside. Add remaining chopped cookies to filling; stir just until blended.
- Spoon into crust. Smooth top lightly with back of spoon to form even layer. Sprinkle with the reserved chopped cookies.

- Serve immediately. Or cover and refrigerate until ready to serve.

Nutrition Information

- Calories: 440
- Total Carbohydrate: 39 g
- Fiber: 1 g
- Cholesterol: 85 mg
- Total Fat: 30 g
- Protein: 6 g
- Sodium: 540 mg
- Sugar: 26 g
- Saturated Fat: 15 g

66. No Bake Orange Cheesecake

Serving: 0 | Prep: 15mins | Cook: 4hours | Ready in: 4hours15mins

Ingredients

- 1 graham cracker, crushed
- 2/3 cup boiling water
- 1 pkg. (0.3 oz.) JELL-O Orange Flavor Sugar Free Gelatin
- 1 cup BREAKSTONE'S or KNUDSEN 2% Milkfat Low Fat Cottage Cheese
- 1 tub (8 oz.) PHILADELPHIA 1/3 Less Fat than Cream Cheese
- 2 cups thawed COOL WHIP Sugar Free Whipped Topping

Direction

- Sprinkle crumbs onto bottom of 8- or 9-inch springform pan sprayed with cooking spray.
- Add boiling water to gelatin mix in large bowl; stir 2 min. until completely dissolved. Cool 5 min.; pour into blender. Add cheeses; blend well. Return to bowl. Gently stir in COOL WHIP; pour into springform pan. Smooth top.

- Refrigerate 4 hours or until set. Loosen cheesecake from side of pan before removing rim.

Nutrition Information

- Calories: 100
- Total Carbohydrate: 10 g
- Cholesterol: 10 mg
- Fiber: 0 g
- Sodium: 310 mg
- Saturated Fat: 3 g
- Sugar: 3 g
- Protein: 8 g
- Total Fat: 3.5 g

67. No Bake Strawberry Banana Smoothie Cheesecake

Serving: 8 | Prep: 15mins | Cook: 1hours | Ready in: 1hours15mins

Ingredients

- 1 cup strawberries
- 1 banana
- 2 pkg. (8 oz. each) PHILADELPHIA Cream Cheese, softened
- 1/3 cup sugar
- 1 tub (8 oz.) COOL WHIP Whipped Topping, thawed
- 1 ready-to-use graham cracker crumb crust (6 oz.)

Direction

- Process fruit in food processor or blender until smooth. Mix cream cheese and sugar in large bowl with mixer until blended. Gently stir in fruit and COOL WHIP.
- Spoon into crust.
- Freeze 4 hours or until firm. Remove from freezer 1 hour before serving to let cheesecake soften slightly.

Nutrition Information

- Calories: 430
- Protein: 5 g
- Total Carbohydrate: 36 g
- Cholesterol: 75 mg
- Fiber: 1 g
- Total Fat: 30 g
- Sodium: 310 mg
- Sugar: 24 g
- Saturated Fat: 19 g

68. OREO Peanut Butter Cheesecake

Serving: 0 | Prep: 20mins | Cook: 5hours | Ready in: 5hours20mins

Ingredients

- 1 pkg. (15.5 oz.) OREO Cookies, divided
- 3 Tbsp. butter or margarine, melted
- 3 pkg. (8 oz. each) PHILADELPHIA Cream Cheese, softened
- 3/4 cup sugar
- 1 container (16 oz.) BREAKSTONE'S or KNUDSEN Sour Cream
- 1 cup creamy peanut butter
- 3 eggs

Direction

- Heat oven to 350°F.
- Crush 16 cookies to form fine crumbs; coarsely chop remaining cookies. Mix crushed cookies and butter; press onto bottom of 9-inch springform pan.
- Beat cream cheese and sugar in large bowl with mixer until blended. Add sour cream and peanut butter; mix well. Add eggs, 1 at a time, mixing on low speed after each just until blended. Gently stir in chopped cookies. Pour over crust.

- Bake 50 min. to 1 hour or until center is almost set. Run knife around rim of pan to loosen cake; cool before removing rim. Refrigerate 4 hours.

Nutrition Information

- Calories: 490
- Total Carbohydrate: 0 g
- Cholesterol: 115 mg
- Sugar: 0 g
- Protein: 10 g
- Saturated Fat: 16 g
- Sodium: 400 mg
- Fiber: 2 g
- Total Fat: 35 g

69. OREO Pumpkin Cheesecake

Serving: 12 | Prep: 15mins | Cook: 5hours55mins | Ready in: 6hours10mins

Ingredients

- 19 OREO Cookies
- 3 pkg. (8 oz. each) PHILADELPHIA Cream Cheese, softened
- 3/4 cup sugar
- 1-1/2 cups canned pumpkin pie filling
- 1 Tbsp. cornstarch
- 3 eggs

Direction

- Heat oven to 325°F.
- Place cookies in single layer on bottom of 9-inch springform pan.
- Beat cream cheese and sugar in large bowl with mixer until blended. Add pumpkin pie filling and cornstarch; mix well. Add eggs, 1 at a time, mixing on low speed after each just until blended. Pour over crust.
- Bake 50 to 55 min. or until center is almost set. Run knife around rim of pan to loosen cake;

cool before removing rim. Refrigerate cheesecake 4 hours.

Nutrition Information

- Calories: 360
- Sugar: 0 g
- Cholesterol: 120 mg
- Saturated Fat: 13 g
- Fiber: 1 g
- Sodium: 310 mg
- Total Carbohydrate: 0 g
- Protein: 6 g
- Total Fat: 24 g

70. Our Best Chocolate Cheesecake

Serving: 16 | Prep: 30mins | Cook: 6hours5mins | Ready in: 6hours35mins

Ingredients

- 18 OREO Cookies, finely crushed (about 1-1/2 cups)
- 2 Tbsp. butter or margarine, melted
- 3 pkg. (8 oz. each) PHILADELPHIA Cream Cheese, softened
- 1 cup sugar
- 1 tsp. vanilla
- 2 pkg. (4 oz. each) BAKER'S Semi-Sweet Chocolate, broken into pieces, melted and cooled
- 3 eggs
- 1-1/2 cups sliced fresh strawberries

Direction

- Heat oven to 325°F.
- Combine cookie crumbs and butter; press onto bottom of 9-inch springform pan. Bake 10 min.
- Beat cream cheese, sugar and vanilla in large bowl with mixer until blended. Add chocolate; mix well. Add eggs, 1 at a time, mixing on low

speed after each just until blended. Pour over crust.

- Bake 45 to 55 min. or until center is almost set. Run knife around rim of pan to loosen cake; cool before removing rim.
- Refrigerate cheesecake 4 hours. Top with strawberries just before serving.

Nutrition Information

- Calories: 370
- Protein: 5 g
- Total Carbohydrate: 28 g
- Fiber: 1 g
- Sodium: 210 mg
- Cholesterol: 80 mg
- Sugar: 23 g
- Saturated Fat: 14 g
- Total Fat: 25 g

71. PHILADELPHIA "Fruit Smoothie" No Bake Cheesecake

Serving: 16 | Prep: 15mins | Cook: 4hours | Ready in: 4hours15mins

Ingredients

- 2 cups graham cracker crumbs
- 6 Tbsp. butter, melted
- 3 Tbsp. sugar
- 4 pkg. (8 oz. each) PHILADELPHIA Neufchatel Cheese, softened
- 3/4 cup sugar
- 1 pkg. (12 oz.) frozen mixed berries (strawberries, raspberries, blueberries, blackberries), thawed, well drained
- 1 tub (8 oz.) COOL WHIP LITE Whipped Topping, thawed

Direction

- Line 13x9-inch pan with Reynolds Wrap® Aluminum Foil, with ends of foil extending over sides. Mix cracker crumbs, butter and 3 Tbsp. sugar; press onto bottom of pan. Refrigerate while preparing filling.

- Beat Neufchatel and 3/4 cup sugar in large bowl with mixer until blended. Add berries; beat on low speed just until blended. Whisk in COOL WHIP. Pour over crust.

- Refrigerate 4 hours or until firm. Use foil handles to lift cheesecake from pan before cutting to serve.

Nutrition Information

- Calories: 320
- Saturated Fat: 13 g
- Total Carbohydrate: 30 g
- Protein: 6 g
- Sugar: 20 g
- Fiber: 1 g
- Cholesterol: 45 mg
- Sodium: 360 mg
- Total Fat: 20 g

---

72. PHILADELPHIA 3 STEP Chocolate Chip Cookie Dough Cheesecake

Serving: 0 | Prep: 10mins | Cook: 3hours40mins | Ready in: 3hours50mins

Ingredients

- 2 pkg. (8 oz. each) PHILADELPHIA Cream Cheese, softened
- 1/2 cup sugar
- 1/2 tsp. vanilla
- 2 eggs
- 3/4 cup prepared or refrigerated chocolate chip cookie dough, divided
- 1 ready-to-use graham cracker crumb crust (6 oz.)

Direction

- Preheat oven to 350°F. Beat cream cheese, sugar and vanilla in large bowl with electric mixer on medium speed until well blended. Add eggs; mix just until blended. Remove 1/2 cup of the dough; drop by teaspoonfuls into batter. Stir gently until well blended.

- Pour into crust. Top with level teaspoonfuls of the remaining 1/4 cup cookie dough.

- Bake 40 minutes or until center is almost set. Cool. Refrigerate 3 hours or overnight. Store leftover cheesecake in refrigerator.

Nutrition Information

- Calories: 540
- Saturated Fat: 13 g
- Total Carbohydrate: 0 g
- Total Fat: 32 g
- Cholesterol: 80 mg
- Fiber: 0 g
- Protein: 6 g
- Sodium: 450 mg
- Sugar: 0 g

---

73. PHILADELPHIA 3 STEP OREO Cheesecake

Serving: 0 | Prep: 10mins | Cook: 40mins | Ready in: 50mins

Ingredients

- 2 pkg. (8 oz. each) PHILADELPHIA Cream Cheese, softened
- 1/2 cup sugar
- 1/2 tsp. vanilla
- 2 eggs
- 6 OREO Cookies, coarsely chopped, divided
- 1 OREO Pie Crust (6 oz.)

Direction

- Heat oven to 325°F.

- Beat cream cheese, sugar and vanilla with mixer until blended. Add eggs; mix just until blended. Stir in 1/2 cup cookies.
- Pour into crust; sprinkle with remaining cookies.
- Bake 35 to 40 min. or until center is almost set. Cool. Refrigerate 3 hours.

Nutrition Information

- Calories: 400
- Sugar: 0 g
- Saturated Fat: 14 g
- Cholesterol: 120 mg
- Sodium: 380 mg
- Fiber: 1 g
- Protein: 6 g
- Total Carbohydrate: 0 g
- Total Fat: 27 g

74. PHILADELPHIA 3 STEP Peppermint Cheesecake

Serving: 8 | Prep: 10mins | Cook: 3hours40mins | Ready in: 3hours50mins

Ingredients

- 2 pkg. (8 oz. each) PHILADELPHIA Cream Cheese, softened
- 1/2 cup sugar
- 1/2 tsp. vanilla
- 2 eggs
- 1 cup finely crushed starlight mints, divided
- 1 ready-to-use graham cracker crumb crust (6 oz.)
- 1 cup thawed COOL WHIP Whipped Topping

Direction

- Heat oven to 350°F.
- Beat cream cheese, sugar and vanilla in large bowl with mixer until blended. Add eggs; mix

just until blended. Stir in 1/2 cup crushed mints.
- Pour into crust; sprinkle with 1/4 cup of the remaining crushed mints.
- Bake 40 min. or until center is almost set. Cool. Refrigerate 3 hours or until firm. Top with COOL WHIP and remaining crushed mints just before serving.

Nutrition Information

- Calories: 500
- Protein: 6 g
- Cholesterol: 120 mg
- Fiber: 0 g
- Total Carbohydrate: 0 g
- Saturated Fat: 16 g
- Total Fat: 27 g
- Sugar: 0 g
- Sodium: 330 mg

75. PHILADELPHIA 3 STEP Pumpkin Cheesecake

Serving: 8 | Prep: 10mins | Cook: 4hours40mins | Ready in: 4hours50mins

Ingredients

- 2 pkg. (8 oz. each) PHILADELPHIA Cream Cheese, softened
- 1/2 cup sugar
- 1/2 cup canned pumpkin
- 1/2 tsp. vanilla
- 1/2 tsp. ground cinnamon
- dash ground cloves
- dash ground nutmeg
- 2 eggs
- 1 ready-to-use graham cracker crumb crust (6 oz.)
- 1 cup thawed COOL WHIP Whipped Topping

Direction

- Heat oven to 350°F.
- Beat cream cheese, sugar, pumpkin, vanilla and spices in large bowl with mixer until blended. Add eggs; beat just until blended.
- Pour into crust.
- Bake 40 min. or until center is almost set. Cool. Refrigerate 3 hours. Top with COOL WHIP just before serving.

Nutrition Information

- Calories: 400
- Total Fat: 28 g
- Sugar: 0 g
- Protein: 6 g
- Cholesterol: 110 mg
- Fiber: 0.8818 g
- Saturated Fat: 15 g
- Sodium: 360 mg
- Total Carbohydrate: 0 g

---

76. PHILADELPHIA 3 Step Chocolate Chip Cheesecake

Serving: 8 | Prep: 10mins | Cook: 3hours40mins | Ready in: 3hours50mins

Ingredients

- 2 pkg. (8 oz. each) PHILADELPHIA Cream Cheese, softened
- 1/2 cup sugar
- 1/2 tsp. vanilla
- 2 eggs
- 3/4 cup miniature semi-sweet chocolate chips, divided
- 1 ready-to-use graham cracker crumb crust (6 oz.)

Direction

- Heat oven to 350°F.
- Beat cream cheese, sugar and vanilla in large bowl with mixer until blended. Add eggs; mix

just until blended. Stir in 1/2 cup chocolate chips.
- Pour into crust. Sprinkle with remaining chocolate chips.
- Bake 40 min. or until center is almost set. Cool. Refrigerate 3 hours.

Nutrition Information

- Calories: 480
- Saturated Fat: 18 g
- Protein: 8 g
- Cholesterol: 110 mg
- Total Carbohydrate: 0 g
- Fiber: 2 g
- Total Fat: 32 g
- Sugar: 0 g
- Sodium: 330 mg

---

77. PHILADELPHIA Black Forest Cheesecake

Serving: 0 | Prep: 15mins | Cook: 4hours40mins | Ready in: 4hours55mins

Ingredients

- 20 OREO Cookies, crushed (about 2 cups)
- 3 Tbsp. butter, melted
- 4 pkg. (8 oz. each) PHILADELPHIA Cream Cheese, softened
- 1 cup sugar
- 1 tsp. vanilla
- 1 cup BREAKSTONE'S or KNUDSEN Sour Cream
- 1-1/2 pkg. (4 oz. each) BAKER'S Semi-Sweet Chocolate (6 oz.), broken into pieces, melted
- 4 eggs
- 2 cups thawed COOL WHIP Whipped Topping
- 1 can (21 oz.) cherry pie filling

Direction

- Heat oven to 325ºF.
- Line 13x9-inch pan with foil, with ends of foil extending over sides. Mix cookie crumbs and butter; press firmly onto bottom of pan. Bake 10 min.
- Beat cream cheese, sugar and vanilla in large bowl with mixer until well blended. Add sour cream and chocolate; mix well. Add eggs, 1 at a time, beating after each just until blended. Pour over crust.
- Bake 40 min. or until center is almost set. Cool. Refrigerate 4 hours. Lift cheesecake from pan, using foil handles. Top with COOL WHIP and pie filling.

Nutrition Information

- Calories: 510
- Protein: 7 g
- Sodium: 330 mg
- Saturated Fat: 20 g
- Sugar: 27 g
- Cholesterol: 125 mg
- Total Carbohydrate: 44 g
- Fiber: 2 g
- Total Fat: 34 g

78. PHILADELPHIA Caramel Nut Cheesecake

Serving: 0 | Prep: 20mins | Cook: 5hours5mins | Ready in: 5hours25mins

Ingredients

- 2 cups graham cracker crumbs
- 1 cup PLANTERS COCKTAIL Peanuts, chopped, divided
- 1-1/4 cups sugar, divided
- 6 Tbsp. butter or margarine, melted
- 4 pkg. (8 oz. each) PHILADELPHIA Cream Cheese, softened
- 2 tsp. vanilla
- 1 cup BREAKSTONE'S or KNUDSEN Sour Cream
- 4 eggs
- 1/4 cup caramel ice cream topping

Direction

- Heat oven to 350ºF.
- Line 13x9-inch pan with foil, with ends of foil extending over sides. Mix crumbs, 1/2 cup nuts, 1/4 cup sugar and butter; press onto bottom of pan. Bake 10 min.
- Meanwhile, beat cream cheese, remaining sugar and vanilla with mixer until well blended. Add sour cream; mix well. Add eggs, 1 at a time, beating after each just until blended. Pour over crust.
- Bake 35 min. or until center is almost set; cool completely. Refrigerate 4 hours. Top with remaining nuts and caramel topping. Use foil handles to lift cheesecake from pan before cutting to serve.

Nutrition Information

- Calories: 460
- Sodium: 390 mg
- Total Carbohydrate: 0 g
- Saturated Fat: 18 g
- Fiber: 1 g
- Total Fat: 33 g
- Cholesterol: 150 mg
- Sugar: 0 g
- Protein: 9 g

79. PHILADELPHIA Classic Cheesecake

Serving: 16 | Prep: 20mins | Cook: 5hours25mins | Ready in: 5hours45mins

Ingredients

- 1-1/2 cups graham cracker crumbs

- 3 Tbsp. sugar
- 1/3 cup butter or margarine, melted
- 4 pkg. (8 oz. each) PHILADELPHIA Cream Cheese, softened
- 1 cup sugar
- 1 tsp. vanilla
- 4 eggs

Direction

- Heat oven to 325°F.
- Combine graham crumbs, 3 Tbsp. sugar and butter; press onto bottom of 9-inch springform pan.
- Beat cream cheese, 1 cup sugar and vanilla with Mixer until blended. Add eggs, 1 at a time, mixing on low speed after each just until blended. Pour over crust.
- Bake 55 min. or until center is almost set. Run knife around rim of pan to loosen cake; cool before removing rim. Refrigerate cheesecake 4 hours.

Nutrition Information

- Calories: 350
- Total Fat: 26 g
- Total Carbohydrate: 0 g
- Sodium: 310 mg
- Fiber: 0 g
- Saturated Fat: 15 g
- Protein: 6 g
- Sugar: 0 g
- Cholesterol: 120 mg

80. PHILADELPHIA Easter Mini Cheesecakes

Serving: 18 | Prep: 20mins | Cook: 3hours | Ready in: 3hours20mins

Ingredients

- 1 cup graham cracker crumbs

- 3/4 cup plus 2 Tbsp. sugar, divided
- 3 Tbsp. butter or margarine, melted
- 3 pkg. (8 oz. each) PHILADELPHIA Cream Cheese, softened
- 1 tsp. vanilla
- 3 eggs
- 1 cup plus 2 Tbsp. BAKER'S ANGEL FLAKE Coconut, toasted
- 54 speckled malted milk eggs (about 9 oz.)

Direction

- Heat oven to 325°F.
- Mix graham crumbs, 2 Tbsp. sugar and butter; press onto bottoms of 18 paper-lined muffin cups.
- Beat cream cheese, vanilla and remaining sugar with mixer until blended. Add eggs, 1 at a time, mixing on low speed after each just until blended. Spoon over crusts.
- Bake 25 to 30 min. or until centers are almost set. Cool completely. Refrigerate 2 hours.
- Top each cheesecake with 1 Tbsp. coconut; shape to resemble bird's nest. Fill with malted milk eggs.

Nutrition Information

- Calories: 320
- Sugar: 0 g
- Fiber: 1 g
- Protein: 5 g
- Total Fat: 22 g
- Cholesterol: 85 mg
- Saturated Fat: 14 g
- Sodium: 230 mg
- Total Carbohydrate: 0 g

81. PHILADELPHIA New York Cheesecake Bars

Serving: 16 | Prep: 15mins | Cook: 5hours10mins | Ready in: 5hours25mins

Ingredients

- 6 graham crackers, finely crushed (about 1 cup)
- 3 Tbsp. sugar
- 3 Tbsp. butter or margarine, melted
- 5 pkg. (8 oz. each) PHILADELPHIA Cream Cheese, softened
- 1 cup sugar
- 3 Tbsp. flour
- 1 Tbsp. vanilla
- 1 cup BREAKSTONE'S or KNUDSEN Sour Cream
- 4 eggs
- 1 can (21 oz.) cherry pie filling

Direction

- Heat oven to 325°F.
- Line 13x9-inch pan with Reynolds Wrap® Aluminum Foil, with ends of foil extending over sides. Mix graham crumbs, 3 Tbsp. sugar and butter; press onto bottom of pan. Bake 10 min.
- Meanwhile, beat cream cheese, 1 cup sugar, flour and vanilla with mixer until blended. Add sour cream; mix well. Add eggs, 1 at a time, mixing on low after each just until blended; pour over crust.
- Bake 40 min. or until center is almost set. Cool completely. Refrigerate 4 hours. Use foil handles to lift cheesecake from pan before cutting to serve. Top with pie filling.

Nutrition Information

- Calories: 450
- Fiber: 0 g
- Sodium: 350 mg
- Protein: 7 g
- Total Carbohydrate: 34 g
- Sugar: 19 g
- Total Fat: 31 g
- Saturated Fat: 18 g
- Cholesterol: 140 mg

82. PHILADELPHIA New York Chocolate Cheesecake

Serving: 0 | Prep: 15mins | Cook: 5hours10mins | Ready in: 5hours25mins

Ingredients

- 25 chocolate wafer cookies, finely crushed (about 1 cup)
- 3 Tbsp. sugar
- 3 Tbsp. butter or margarine, melted
- 5 pkg. (8 oz. each) PHILADELPHIA Cream Cheese, softened
- 1 cup sugar
- 3 Tbsp. flour
- 1 Tbsp. vanilla
- 2 pkg. (4 oz. each) BAKER'S Semi-Sweet Chocolate, broken into pieces, melted, slightly cooled
- 1 cup BREAKSTONE'S or KNUDSEN Sour Cream
- 3 eggs

Direction

- Preheat oven to 350°F if using a silver 9-inch springform pan (or to 325°F if using a dark nonstick 9-inch springform pan). Mix crumbs, 3 Tbsp. sugar and the butter; press firmly onto bottom of pan. Bake 10 min.
- Beat cream cheese, 1 cup sugar, the flour and vanilla in large bowl with electric mixer on medium speed until well blended. Add melted chocolate and sour cream; mix well. Add eggs, one at a time, mixing on low speed after each addition just until blended. Pour over crust.
- Bake 1 hour 5 min. to 1 hour 10 min. or until center is almost set. Run knife around rim of pan to loosen cake; cool before removing rim of pan. Refrigerate at least 4 hours or overnight. Store leftover cheesecake in refrigerator.

Nutrition Information

- Calories: 500
- Saturated Fat: 22 g
- Cholesterol: 130 mg
- Fiber: 2 g
- Protein: 8 g
- Total Fat: 36 g
- Sodium: 380 mg
- Total Carbohydrate: 35 g
- Sugar: 27 g

83. PHILADELPHIA New York Style Strawberry Swirl Cheesecake

Serving: 16 | Prep: 15mins | Cook: 5hours20mins | Ready in: 5hours35mins

Ingredients

- 1 cup graham cracker crumbs
- 3 Tbsp. sugar
- 3 Tbsp. butter, melted
- 5 pkg. (8 oz. each) PHILADELPHIA Cream Cheese, softened
- 1 cup sugar
- 3 Tbsp. flour
- 1 Tbsp. vanilla
- 1 cup BREAKSTONE'S or KNUDSEN Sour Cream
- 4 eggs
- 1/3 cup seedless strawberry jam

Direction

- Heat oven to 325°F.
- Line 13x9-inch pan with Reynolds Wrap® Aluminum Foil, with ends of foil extending over sides. Combine graham crumbs, 3 Tbsp. sugar and butter; press onto bottom of prepared pan. Bake 10 min.
- Beat cream cheese, 1 cup sugar, flour and vanilla with mixer until blended. Add sour cream; mix well. Add eggs, 1 at a time, mixing on low speed after each just until blended.

Pour over crust. Gently drop small spoonfuls of jam over batter; swirl gently with knife.
- Bake 40 min. or until center is almost set. Cool completely. Refrigerate 4 hours. Use foil handles to lift cheesecake from pan before cutting to serve.

Nutrition Information

- Calories: 410
- Sodium: 340 mg
- Sugar: 0 g
- Fiber: 0 g
- Cholesterol: 155 mg
- Saturated Fat: 18 g
- Total Carbohydrate: 0 g
- Total Fat: 30 g
- Protein: 7 g

84. PHILADELPHIA No Bake Cheesecake

Serving: 8 | Prep: 15mins | Cook: 3hours25mins | Ready in: 3hours40mins

Ingredients

- 8 graham crackers, finely crushed (about 1-1/3 cups)
- 6 Tbsp. granular no-calorie sweetener, divided
- 3 Tbsp. margarine, melted
- 1 pkg. (8 oz.) PHILADELPHIA Neufchatel Cheese, softened
- 1-1/2 cups thawed COOL WHIP Sugar Free Whipped Topping
- 1 cup sliced fresh strawberries
- 3 kiwis, peeled, sliced

Direction

- Heat oven to 375°F.
- Combine graham crumbs, 2 Tbsp. granulated sweetener and margarine; press onto bottom

and up side of 9-inch pie plate. Bake 8 to 10 min. or until lightly browned; cool completely.

- Mix Neufchatel and remaining granulated sweetener in medium bowl until blended. Gently stir in COOL WHIP; spoon into crust. Refrigerate 3 hours.
- Top with fruit before serving.

Nutrition Information

- Calories: 230
- Total Carbohydrate: 0 g
- Fiber: 2 g
- Saturated Fat: 7 g
- Sugar: 0 g
- Protein: 4 g
- Total Fat: 14 g
- Sodium: 260 mg
- Cholesterol: 20 mg

85. PHILADELPHIA No Bake Peach Cheesecake

Serving: 16 | Prep: 15mins | Cook: 4hours | Ready in: 4hours15mins

Ingredients

- 2 cups graham cracker crumbs
- 6 Tbsp. margarine, melted
- 1 cup sugar, divided
- 4 pkg. (8 oz. each) PHILADELPHIA Neufchatel Cheese, softened
- 1 pkg. (3 oz.) JELL-O Peach Flavor Gelatin
- 1 tub (8 oz.) COOL WHIP LITE Whipped Topping, thawed
- 2 fresh peaches, chopped

Direction

- Combine graham crumbs, margarine and 1/4 cup sugar; press onto bottom of 13x9-inch pan. Refrigerate until ready to use.

- Beat Neufchatel and remaining sugar in large bowl with mixer until blended. Add dry gelatin mix; mix well. Stir in COOL WHIP and peaches. Pour over crust.
- Refrigerate 4 hours or until firm.

Nutrition Information

- Calories: 340
- Fiber: 1 g
- Total Fat: 20 g
- Total Carbohydrate: 35 g
- Protein: 6 g
- Saturated Fat: 11 g
- Cholesterol: 35 mg
- Sugar: 25 g
- Sodium: 390 mg

86. PHILADELPHIA Peanut Butter Chocolate Cheesecake

Serving: 16 | Prep: 20mins | Cook: 5hours50mins | Ready in: 6hours10mins

Ingredients

- 16 peanut butter sandwich cookies, finely crushed (about 2 cups)
- 3 Tbsp. butter, melted
- 4 pkg. (8 oz. each) PHILADELPHIA Cream Cheese, softened
- 1 cup sugar
- 1 Tbsp. vanilla
- 1 cup BREAKSTONE'S or KNUDSEN Sour Cream
- 1/2 cup creamy peanut butter
- 4 eggs
- 2 oz. BAKER'S Semi-Sweet Chocolate

Direction

- Heat oven to 325°F.
- Line 13x9-inch pan with foil, with ends of foil extending over sides. Mix cookie crumbs and

butter; press onto bottom of prepared pan. Bake 10 min.

- Beat cream cheese, sugar and vanilla in large bowl with mixer until blended. Add sour cream and peanut butter; mix well. Add eggs, 1 at a time, mixing on low speed after each just until blended; pour over crust.
- Bake 40 min. or until center is almost set. Cool. Refrigerate 4 hours.
- Melt chocolate as directed on package; drizzle over cheesecake. Refrigerate 15 min. or until chocolate is firm. Use foil handles to remove cheesecake from pan before cutting to serve.

Nutrition Information

- Calories: 430
- Sodium: 340 mg
- Protein: 9 g
- Fiber: 1 g
- Cholesterol: 140 mg
- Total Carbohydrate: 0 g
- Sugar: 0 g
- Total Fat: 33 g
- Saturated Fat: 17 g

87. PHILADELPHIA OREO No Bake Cheesecake

Serving: 16 | Prep: 15mins | Cook: 4hours | Ready in: 4hours15mins

Ingredients

- 36 OREO Cookies, divided
- 1/4 cup butter, melted
- 4 pkg. (8 oz. each) PHILADELPHIA Cream Cheese, softened
- 3/4 cup sugar
- 1 tsp. vanilla
- 1 tub (8 oz.) COOL WHIP Whipped Topping, thawed

Direction

- Chop 15 cookies coarsely. Finely crush remaining cookies; mix with butter. Press onto bottom of 13x9-inch pan. Refrigerate until ready to use.
- Beat cream cheese, sugar and vanilla in large bowl with mixer until blended. Gently stir in COOL WHIP and chopped cookies; spoon over crust.
- Refrigerate 4 hours or until firm.

Nutrition Information

- Calories: 410
- Saturated Fat: 17 g
- Total Carbohydrate: 33 g
- Fiber: 1 g
- Sugar: 24 g
- Protein: 5 g
- Cholesterol: 85 mg
- Total Fat: 29 g
- Sodium: 350 mg

88. PHILADELPHIA® 3 STEP® Macaroon Cheesecake

Serving: 0 | Prep: 10mins | Cook: 3hours40mins | Ready in: 3hours50mins

Ingredients

- 2 cups soft coconut macaroon cookie crumbs
- 2 Tbsp. butter or margarine, melted
- 2 pkg. (8 oz. each) PHILADELPHIA Cream Cheese, softened
- 1/2 cup sugar
- 1/2 tsp. imitation vanilla
- 2 eggs
- 1 cup sliced strawberries

Direction

- Preheat oven to 350°F. Mix crumbs and butter. Press firmly onto bottom and up side of greased 9-inch pie plate. Beat cream cheese, sugar and vanilla in large bowl with electric mixer on medium speed until well blended. Add eggs; mix just until blended.

- Pour into crust.
- Bake 40 minutes or until center is almost set. Cool. Refrigerate 3 hours or overnight. Top with strawberries just before serving.

Nutrition Information

- Calories: 410
- Protein: 7 g
- Sugar: 0 g
- Saturated Fat: 19 g
- Total Carbohydrate: 0 g
- Fiber: 1 g
- Total Fat: 30 g
- Cholesterol: 150 mg
- Sodium: 270 mg

89. PHILADELPHIA® 3 STEP® Pina Colada Cheesecake

Serving: 0 | Prep: 10mins | Cook: 3hours40mins | Ready in: 3hours50mins

Ingredients

- 2 pkg. (8 oz. each) PHILADELPHIA Cream Cheese, softened
- 1/2 cup sugar
- 1/2 tsp. vanilla
- 2 eggs
- 1/3 cup thawed frozen piña colada tropical fruit mixer concentrate
- 1 ready-to-use graham cracker crumb crust (6 oz.)
- 1/4 cup BAKER'S ANGEL FLAKE Coconut
- 4 canned pineapple rings, drained

Direction

- Preheat oven to 350°F. Beat cream cheese, sugar and vanilla with electric mixer on

medium speed until well blended. Add eggs; mix just until blended. Stir in fruit mixer concentrate.

- Pour into crust.
- Bake 40 min. or until center is almost set. Cool. Refrigerate at least 3 hours before serving. Top with coconut and pineapple. Store leftover cheesecake in refrigerator.

Nutrition Information

- Calories: 440
- Sugar: 0 g
- Total Fat: 28 g
- Cholesterol: 115 mg
- Fiber: 1 g
- Sodium: 350 mg
- Total Carbohydrate: 0 g
- Saturated Fat: 16 g
- Protein: 6 g

90. PHILLY OREO Cheesecake Recipe

Serving: 16 | Prep: 20mins | Cook: 5hours45mins | Ready in: 6hours5mins

Ingredients

- 36 OREO Cookies, divided
- 1/4 cup butter or margarine, melted
- 4 pkg. (8 oz. each) PHILADELPHIA Cream Cheese, softened
- 1 cup sugar
- 1 tsp. vanilla
- 1 cup BREAKSTONE'S or KNUDSEN Sour Cream
- 4 eggs

Direction

- Heat oven to 325°F.
- Line 13x9-inch pan with Reynolds Wrap® Aluminum Foil, with ends of foil extending

over sides. Process 28 cookies in food processor until finely ground. Add butter; mix well. Press onto bottom of prepared pan.

- Beat cream cheese, sugar and vanilla in large bowl with mixer until blended. Add sour cream; mix well. Add eggs, 1 at a time, beating after each just until blended. Chop remaining cookies; stir 1-1/2 cups into batter. Pour over crust; top with remaining chopped cookies.
- Bake 45 min. or until center is almost set. Cool completely. Refrigerate 4 hours. Use foil handles to lift cheesecake from pan before cutting to serve.

Nutrition Information

- Calories: 460
- Saturated Fat: 18 g
- Fiber: 1 g
- Cholesterol: 150 mg
- Sugar: 0 g
- Total Fat: 32 g
- Protein: 7 g
- Total Carbohydrate: 0 g
- Sodium: 430 mg

91. PLANTERS Almond Cheesecake

Serving: 0 | Prep: 20mins | Cook: 4hours55mins | Ready in: 5hours15mins

Ingredients

- 1-1/2 cups PLANTERS Sliced Almonds, toasted, divided
- 3/4 cup graham cracker crumbs
- 1/4 cup (1/2 stick) butter, melted
- 3 pkg. (8 oz. each) PHILADELPHIA Cream Cheese, softened
- 3/4 cup sugar
- 1/2 cup BREAKSTONE'S or KNUDSEN Sour Cream
- 2 Tbsp. almond-flavored liqueur

- 3 eggs

Direction

- Preheat oven to 325°F if using a silver 9-inch springform pan (or to 300°F if using a dark nonstick 9-inch springform pan). Finely chop 1 cup of the almonds; mix with graham crumbs and butter. Press firmly onto bottom of pan. Bake 8 min; cool completely.
- Beat cream cheese and sugar in large bowl with electric mixer on medium speed until well blended. Add sour cream and liqueur; mix well. Add eggs, one at a time, beating on low speed after each addition just until blended. Pour over crust.
- Bake 50 to 55 min. or until center is almost set. Run knife or metal spatula around side of pan to loosen cake; cool before removing side of pan. Refrigerate at least 4 hours or overnight. Sprinkle with remaining 1/2 cup almonds just before serving. Store any leftover cheesecake in refrigerator.

Nutrition Information

- Calories: 340
- Fiber: 2 g
- Protein: 7 g
- Total Fat: 27 g
- Sodium: 220 mg
- Saturated Fat: 12 g
- Sugar: 0 g
- Total Carbohydrate: 0 g
- Cholesterol: 110 mg

92. Passion Fruit Cheesecake

Serving: 16 | Prep: 30mins | Cook: 6hours15mins | Ready in: 6hours45mins

Ingredients

- 1 cup graham cracker crumbs
- 1-2/3 cups sugar, divided

- 3 Tbsp. butter, melted
- 4 pkg. (8 oz. each) PHILADELPHIA Cream Cheese, softened
- 2 Tbsp. flour
- 4 eggs
- 1 pkg. (14 oz.) frozen passion fruit pulp, thawed, divided
- 1 cup halved strawberries
- 1 kiwi

Direction

- HEAT oven to 325°F.
- Mix graham crumbs, 3 Tbsp. sugar and butter; press onto bottom of 9-inch springform pan. Bake 10 min.
- Beat cream cheese, flour and 1 cup of the remaining sugar in large bowl with mixer until blended. Add eggs, 1 at a time, mixing on low speed after each just until blended. Stir in 1/2 cup passion fruit; pour over crust.
- Bake 1 hour 5 min. or until center is almost set. Run knife around rim of pan to loosen cake; cool before removing rim. Refrigerate cheesecake 4 hours.
- Meanwhile, bring remaining passion fruit and sugar just to boil in saucepan on medium-low heat 15 min. or until thickened, stirring frequently. Cool completely.
- Cut kiwi into thin slices. Add to top of cheesecake along with the strawberries. Drizzle with passion fruit sauce.

Nutrition Information

- Calories: 350
- Protein: 6 g
- Total Carbohydrate: 0 g
- Sodium: 280 mg
- Saturated Fat: 13 g
- Total Fat: 23 g
- Cholesterol: 125 mg
- Fiber: 1 g
- Sugar: 0 g

93. Peanut Butter Mini Cheesecakes

Serving: 12 | Prep: 20mins | Cook: 3hours | Ready in: 3hours20mins

Ingredients

- 1 cup graham cracker crumbs
- 3/4 cup plus 3 Tbsp. sugar, divided
- 3 Tbsp. butter or margarine, melted
- 3 pkg. (8 oz. each) PHILADELPHIA Cream Cheese, softened
- 1 tsp. vanilla
- 1/2 cup creamy peanut butter
- 1/4 cup milk
- 3 eggs

Direction

- Heat oven to 325°F.
- Mix graham crumbs, 3 Tbsp. sugar and butter until blended; press onto bottoms of 12 paper-lined muffin cups.
- Beat cream cheese, remaining sugar and vanilla with mixer until blended. Add peanut butter and milk; mix well. Add eggs, 1 at a time, mixing on low speed after each just until blended. Spoon over crusts.
- Bake 25 to 30 min. or until centers are almost set. Cool completely. Refrigerate 2 hours.

Nutrition Information

- Calories: 390
- Total Carbohydrate: 0 g
- Fiber: 1 g
- Sugar: 0 g
- Protein: 8 g
- Saturated Fat: 15 g
- Sodium: 360 mg
- Total Fat: 28 g
- Cholesterol: 130 mg

94. Peppermint Bark Cheesecake

Serving: 16 | Prep: 35mins | Cook: 6hours |Ready in: 6hours35mins

Ingredients

- 18 vanilla creme-filled chocolate sandwich cookies, finely crushed (about 1-1/2 cups)
- 3 Tbsp. butter, melted
- 30 starlight mints, divided
- 4 pkg. (8 oz. each) PHILADELPHIA Cream Cheese, softened
- 1 cup sugar
- 4 eggs
- 1 pkg. (4 oz.) BAKER'S White Chocolate, melted
- 1/4 tsp. peppermint extract
- 1 pkg. (4 oz.) BAKER'S Semi-Sweet Chocolate, divided
- 2 cups thawed COOL WHIP Whipped Topping

Direction

- Heat oven to 325°F.
- Mix cookie crumbs and butter until blended; press onto bottom of 9-inch springform pan. Bake 10 min.
- Meanwhile, crush 25 mints. Beat cream cheese and sugar in large bowl with mixer until blended. Add eggs, 1 at a time, mixing on low speed after each just until blended. Add white chocolate, crushed mints and extract; mix just until blended. Chop half the semi-sweet chocolate; stir into batter. Pour over crust.
- Bake 55 min. to 1 hour or until center is almost set. Run knife around rim of pan to loosen cake; cool before removing rim. Refrigerate 4 hours. Meanwhile, crush remaining mints; chop remaining semi-sweet chocolate.
- Spread cheesecake with 1 cup COOL WHIP just before serving. Drop remaining COOL WHIP in dollops around edge of cheesecake. Sprinkle remaining crushed mints and chopped chocolate over center of cheesecake.

Nutrition Information

- Calories: 470
- Protein: 6 g
- Saturated Fat: 18 g
- Sodium: 320 mg
- Cholesterol: 130 mg
- Sugar: 0 g
- Total Carbohydrate: 0 g
- Fiber: 1 g
- Total Fat: 31 g

95. Pineapple No Bake Cheesecake Dessert

Serving: 16 | Prep: 15mins | Cook: 4hours |Ready in: 4hours15mins

Ingredients

- 1 can (20 oz.) crushed pineapple in juice, undrained
- 1 pkg. (3.4 oz.) JELL-O Vanilla Flavor Instant Pudding
- 1 tub (8 oz.) COOL WHIP Whipped Topping, thawed, divided
- 2 pkg. (8 oz. each) PHILADELPHIA Cream Cheese, softened
- 1/3 cup sugar
- 1 angel food cake (10 oz.), cut into 1-inch cubes
- 6 strawberries, quartered lengthwise

Direction

- Whisk pineapple and dry pudding mix in medium bowl until blended. Stir in 1 cup COOL WHIP.
- Mix cream cheese and sugar in large bowl until blended. Gently stir in remaining COOL WHIP.
- Place half the cake cubes in 9-inch springform pan; top with layers of cream cheese mixture and remaining cake cubes. Cover with pineapple mixture.

- Refrigerate 4 hours. Remove rim of pan. Serve dessert topped with strawberries.

Nutrition Information

- Calories: 240
- Total Fat: 13 g
- Sugar: 0 g
- Cholesterol: 30 mg
- Sodium: 340 mg
- Fiber: 0.6675 g
- Protein: 3 g
- Saturated Fat: 9 g
- Total Carbohydrate: 0 g

96. Pineapple Upside Down Cheesecake

Serving: 16 | Prep: 15mins | Cook: 4hours40mins | Ready in: 4hours55mins

Ingredients

- 2 Tbsp. brown sugar
- 5 Tbsp. butter, melted, divided
- 2 cans (8 oz. each) pineapple slices in juice, well drained
- 7 maraschino cherries, well drained, stemmed
- 1 cup graham cracker crumbs
- 3/4 cup plus 3 Tbsp. granulated sugar, divided
- 3 pkg. (8 oz. each) PHILADELPHIA Cream Cheese, softened
- 3/4 cup BREAKSTONE'S or KNUDSEN Sour Cream
- 2 tsp. vanilla
- 3 eggs

Direction

- Heat oven to 325°F.
- Mix brown sugar and 2 Tbsp. butter in 9-inch round pan until blended; spread to evenly cover bottom of pan. Top with pineapple slices, cutting if necessary to make even layer. Place cherries in centers of pineapple slices.
- Combine graham crumbs, 3 Tbsp. granulated sugar and remaining butter; press gently into tops of pineapple slices.
- Beat cream cheese and remaining granulated sugar with Mixer until blended. Add sour cream and vanilla; mix well. Add eggs, 1 at a time, beating on low speed after each just until blended; pour over pineapple.
- Bake 55 min. to 1 hour or until center is almost set. Run knife around side of pan to loosen cake; cool completely. Invert cheesecake onto plate; carefully remove pan. Refrigerate cheesecake 3 hours.

Nutrition Information

- Calories: 300
- Fiber: 1 g
- Sugar: 0 g
- Total Fat: 21 g
- Saturated Fat: 12 g
- Sodium: 240 mg
- Cholesterol: 110 mg
- Total Carbohydrate: 0 g
- Protein: 5 g

97. Pumpkin Cheesecake

Serving: 8 | Prep: 10mins | Cook: 55mins | Ready in: 1hours5mins

Ingredients

- 2 pkg. (8 oz. each) PHILADELPHIA Cream Cheese, softened
- 1 cup canned pumpkin puree
- 1/2 cup brown sugar
- 1 tsp. vanilla
- 2 eggs
- 1 (6 oz.) ready-to-use graham cracker crumb crust (or make your own)

Direction

- Preheat oven at 325 degrees.
- Beat cream cheese, pumpkin, sugar, and vanilla together until well-blended. Add two eggs and mix in well.
- Pour cheesecake mixture onto graham cracker crust, and bake at 325 for 55 minutes (or until the center feels almost set).
- Take cheesecake out of oven and let cool, then refrigerate for at least four hours before serving.

Nutrition Information

- Calories: 0 g
- Saturated Fat: 0 g
- Fiber: 0 g
- Cholesterol: 0 g
- Sodium: 0 g
- Total Carbohydrate: 0 g
- Protein: 0 g
- Sugar: 0 g
- Total Fat: 0 g

98. Pumpkin Dump Cake With Pudding Topping

Serving: 15 | Prep: 15mins | Cook: 1hours | Ready in: 1hours15mins

Ingredients

- 15 oz. can pumpkin puree
- 1 cup evaporated milk
- 3/4 cup sugar
- 2 eggs
- 1 tsp. ground cinnamon
- 1/2 tsp. ground nutmeg
- 1 tsp. vanilla
- 1 box (16.5-oz.) yellow cake mix
- 1-1/2 sticks butter, melted
- 1 pkg. (3 oz.) JELL-O Cheesecake Flavor Instant Pudding
- 1 cup milk
- 1 tub (8 oz.) COOL WHIP Whipped Topping, thawed

Direction

- To Make Cake
- In mixing bowl, combine pumpkin, evaporated milk, sugar, eggs, cinnamon, nutmeg and vanilla. *Line the bottom and sides of a 13"x 9" baking pan with waxed paper, and then pour in the pumpkin mixture.
- Sprinkle dry cake mix over pumpkin. Spoon melted butter over cake mix.
- Bake at 350 degrees for 50-60 minutes or until golden brown in color. Let stand about 10 minutes, then flip dessert over and out of pan onto serving dish or into another 13" x 9" baking pan. Carefully remove waxed paper. Let cool completely; refrigerate.
- To Make Topping
- Whisk together pudding mix and 1 cup milk for 2 minutes. Let sit in fridge for about 5 minutes to thicken. Carefully fold in COOL WHIP to combine. Spread over the top of dessert. Keep refrigerated.

Nutrition Information

- Calories: 0 g
- Cholesterol: 0 g
- Total Carbohydrate: 0 g
- Protein: 0 g
- Sugar: 0 g
- Saturated Fat: 0 g
- Fiber: 0 g
- Total Fat: 0 g
- Sodium: 0 g

99. Pumpkin Spiced Cheesecake

Serving: 16 | Prep: 45mins | Cook: 5hours15mins | Ready in: 6hours

Ingredients

- 38 gingersnaps, finely crushed (about 1-1/2 cups)
- 1/4 cup finely chopped PLANTERS Walnuts
- 1/4 cup butter or margarine, melted
- 4 pkg. (8 oz. each) PHILADELPHIA Cream Cheese, softened
- 1 cup sugar
- 3 Tbsp. flour
- 1 container (8 oz.) BREAKSTONE'S or KNUDSEN Sour Cream
- 1 cup mashed cooked fresh pumpkin
- 1 Tbsp. pumpkin pie spice
- 1 tsp. vanilla
- 4 eggs

Direction

- Heat oven to 325°F.
- Combine cookie crumbs, nuts and butter; press onto bottom and 1 inch up side of 9-inch springform pan.
- Beat cream cheese, sugar and flour in large bowl with mixer until blended. Add sour cream, pumpkin, pumpkin pie spice and vanilla; mix well. Add eggs, 1 at a time, mixing on low speed after each just until blended. Pour into crust.
- Bake 1 hour 15 min. or until center is almost set. Run knife around rim of pan to loosen cake; cool before removing rim. Refrigerate cheesecake 4 hours.

Nutrition Information

- Calories: 400
- Protein: 7 g
- Sodium: 370 mg
- Sugar: 0 g
- Fiber: 1 g
- Cholesterol: 140 mg
- Total Fat: 28 g
- Total Carbohydrate: 0 g
- Saturated Fat: 16 g

100. Pumpkin Swirl Cheesecake

Serving: 16 | Prep: 20mins | Cook: 5hours45mins | Ready in: 6hours5mins

Ingredients

- 25 gingersnaps, finely crushed (about 1-1/2 cups)
- 1/2 cup finely chopped PLANTERS Pecans
- 1/4 cup butter, melted
- 4 pkg. (8 oz. each) PHILADELPHIA Cream Cheese, softened
- 1 cup sugar, divided
- 1 tsp. vanilla
- 4 eggs
- 1 cup canned pumpkin
- 1 tsp. ground cinnamon
- 1/4 tsp. ground nutmeg
- dash ground cloves

Direction

- Heat oven to 325°F.
- Combine gingersnap crumbs, nuts and butter; press onto bottom of 13x9-inch pan.
- Beat cream cheese, 3/4 cup sugar and vanilla with mixer until blended. Add eggs, 1 at a time, beating on low speed after each just until blended. Remove 1-1/2 cups batter; set aside. Stir remaining sugar, pumpkin and spices into remaining batter.
- Pour half the pumpkin batter over crust; top with spoonfuls of half the plain batter. Repeat layers; swirl gently with knife.
- Bake 45 min. or until center is almost set. Cool completely. Refrigerate 4 hours.

Nutrition Information

- Calories: 370
- Protein: 6 g
- Cholesterol: 115 mg
- Fiber: 0.9141 g

- Total Fat: 27 g
- Total Carbohydrate: 0 g
- Sugar: 0 g
- Saturated Fat: 14 g
- Sodium: 330 mg

101. Quick Cheesecake

Serving: 8 | Prep: 5mins | Cook: | Ready in: 5mins

Ingredients

- 1 tub (24.2 oz.) PHILADELPHIA Ready-To-Eat Cheesecake Filling
- 1 ready-to-use graham cracker crumb crust (6 oz.)

Direction

- Spoon cheesecake filling into crust. Smooth top lightly with back of spoon to form even layer.
- Serve immediately or refrigerate until ready to serve.

Nutrition Information

- Calories: 370
- Fiber: 1 g
- Total Fat: 27 g
- Sodium: 410 mg
- Saturated Fat: 16 g
- Protein: 5 g
- Sugar: 18 g
- Total Carbohydrate: 27 g
- Cholesterol: 85 mg

102. Quick Mini Pudding Cheesecakes

Serving: 0 | Prep: 10mins | Cook: | Ready in: 10mins

Ingredients

- 1 pkg. (4-serving size) JELL-O Vanilla Flavor Instant Pudding
- 1 tub (24.2 oz.) PHILADELPHIA No Bake Cheesecake Filling Original
- 3 pkg. (4 oz. each) mini graham cracker pie crusts (18 shells)
- 1/4 cup multi-colored sprinkles

Direction

- Prepare pudding in large bowl as directed on package. Stir in cheesecake filling until well blended.
- Spoon evenly into pie crusts. Smooth tops lightly with back of spoon to form even layer; top with sprinkles.
- Serve immediately. Or cover and refrigerate until ready to serve. Store leftovers in refrigerator.

Nutrition Information

- Calories: 240
- Total Fat: 13 g
- Saturated Fat: 6 g
- Total Carbohydrate: 0 g
- Protein: 2 g
- Fiber: 0 g
- Sodium: 310 mg
- Cholesterol: 20 mg
- Sugar: 0 g

103. Refrigerated Cranberry Cheesecake

Serving: 8 | Prep: 25mins | Cook: 1hours | Ready in: 1hours25mins

Ingredients

- 1-1/2 cups fresh cranberries, divided
- 1/2 cup PLANTERS Pecan Pieces
- 5 Tbsp. sugar, divided

- 1 pkg. (11.1 oz.) JELL-O No Bake Real Cheesecake Dessert
- 5 Tbsp. margarine, melted
- 1-1/2 cups milk
- 3/4 cup thawed COOL WHIP Whipped Topping

Direction

- Reserve 1/2 cup of the cranberries for garnish. Finely chop remaining 1 cup cranberries; place in medium bowl. Add pecans and 2 Tbsp. of the sugar; mix lightly. Set aside.
- Mix Crust Mix, margarine and remaining 3 Tbsp. sugar. Press firmly onto bottom and up side of 9-inch pie plate. Beat milk and Filling Mix in large bowl with electric mixer on low speed until well blended. Beat on medium speed 3 minutes. (Filling will be thick.) Spread half of the filling into crust. Gently stir cranberry mixture into remaining filling; spread over layer in crust. Refrigerate at least 1 hour.
- Top with whipped topping and reserved cranberries just before serving. Garnish with mint leaves, if desired. Store leftover cheesecake in refrigerator.

Nutrition Information

- Calories: 360
- Protein: 4 g
- Sugar: 32 g
- Total Fat: 18 g
- Saturated Fat: 6 g
- Total Carbohydrate: 47 g
- Fiber: 2 g
- Cholesterol: 5 mg
- Sodium: 390 mg

104.   Rice Pudding Cheesecake

Serving: 16 | Prep: 15mins | Cook: 6hours10mins | Ready in: 6hours25mins

Ingredients

- 40 vanilla wafers, finely crushed (about 1-1/3 cups)
- 1/4 cup butter, melted
- 2 Tbsp. sugar
- 4 pkg. (8 oz. each) PHILADELPHIA Cream Cheese, softened
- 1 cup sugar
- 1 cup BREAKSTONE'S or KNUDSEN Sour Cream
- 1 Tbsp. ground Mexican cinnamon (canela)
- 1 tsp. vanilla
- 4 eggs
- 2-3/4 cups cooked long-grain white rice
- 1/3 cup cajeta (goat milk caramel)

Direction

- Heat oven to 325°F.
- Mix first 3 ingredients; press onto bottom of 9-inch springform pan.
- Beat cream cheese and 1 cup sugar in large bowl with mixer until blended. Add sour cream, cinnamon and vanilla; mix well. Add eggs, 1 at a time, beating on low speed after each just until blended. Stir in rice; pour over crust.
- Bake 1 hour 10 min. or until center is almost set. Run knife around rim of pan to loosen cake; cool before removing rim. Refrigerate cheesecake 4 hours.
- Serve topped with cajeta.

Nutrition Information

- Calories: 420
- Total Carbohydrate: 0 g
- Cholesterol: 140 mg
- Sodium: 310 mg
- Protein: 7 g
- Total Fat: 28 g
- Saturated Fat: 16 g
- Fiber: 1 g
- Sugar: 0 g

105. Roasted Strawberry Pistachio Mini Cheesecakes

Serving: 12 | Prep: 15mins | Cook: 3hours5mins | Ready in: 3hours20mins

Ingredients

- 10 square shortbread cookies (1-1/2 inch)
- 1/3 cup pistachios, chopped, divided
- 1 Tbsp. butter, melted
- 2 pkg. (8 oz. each) PHILADELPHIA Cream Cheese, softened
- 1/2 cup plus 2 Tbsp. sugar, divided
- 1-1/4 tsp. vanilla, divided
- 2 eggs
- 1-1/2 cups small fresh strawberries, cut in half

Direction

- Heat oven to 325°F.
- Use pulsing action of food processor to process cookies and 1/4 cup nuts until finely crushed; spoon into medium bowl. Add butter; mix well. Press onto bottoms of 12 paper-lined muffin cups, adding about 2 tsp. crumb mixture to each cup.
- Beat cream cheese, 1/2 cup sugar and 1 tsp. vanilla in large bowl with mixer until blended. Add eggs, 1 at a time, mixing on low speed after each just until blended. Spoon over crusts.
- Bake 17 to 20 min. or until centers are almost set. Cool completely.
- Meanwhile, increase oven temperature to 350°F. Toss strawberries with remaining sugar and vanilla. Place, with sides touching, on parchment-covered rimmed baking sheet. Bake 15 to 20 min. or until tender and juices are released. Cool completely.
- Refrigerate cheesecake 2 hours. Meanwhile, store cooled strawberries in airtight container at room temperature until ready to use.
- Top cheesecakes with strawberries and remaining nuts just before serving.

Nutrition Information

- Calories: 250
- Cholesterol: 75 mg
- Fiber: 0.861 g
- Protein: 4 g
- Total Carbohydrate: 18 g
- Total Fat: 18 g
- Sugar: 14 g
- Saturated Fat: 9 g
- Sodium: 200 mg

106. Smart Choice Creamy Pumpkin Pie

Serving: 8 | Prep: 10mins | Cook: 3hours40mins | Ready in: 3hours50mins

Ingredients

- 1 pkg. (8 oz.) PHILADELPHIA Neufchatel Cheese, softened
- 1/2 cup granulated sugar
- 1 cup BREAKSTONE'S Reduced Fat or KNUDSEN Light Sour Cream, divided
- 1/2 cup canned pumpkin
- 1/2 tsp. vanilla
- 1/2 tsp. pumpkin pie spice
- 2 eggs
- 1 ready-to-use reduced-fat graham cracker crumb crust (6 oz.)
- 1 Tbsp. brown sugar

Direction

- Heat oven to 350°F.
- Beat Neufchatel and granulated sugar in large bowl with mixer until blended. Add 3/4 cup sour cream, pumpkin, vanilla and spice; mix until blended. Add eggs, 1 at a time, mixing on low speed after each just until blended. Pour into crust.
- Bake 40 min. or until center is almost set. Cool. Refrigerate 3 hours or until chilled.

- Mix remaining sour cream and brown sugar; spoon over cheesecake just before serving.

Nutrition Information

- Calories: 290
- Cholesterol: 80 mg
- Sugar: 0 g
- Sodium: 260 mg
- Total Carbohydrate: 0 g
- Fiber: 1 g
- Saturated Fat: 7 g
- Total Fat: 14 g
- Protein: 7 g

---

107. Spiced Maple Walnut Cheesecake

Serving: 16 | Prep: 30mins | Cook: 6hours10mins | Ready in: 6hours40mins

Ingredients

- 8 graham crackers
- 1 cup chopped PLANTERS Walnuts, toasted, divided
- 1/2 cup plus 2 Tbsp. packed brown sugar, divided
- 2 Tbsp. butter, melted
- 4 pkg. (8 oz. each) PHILADELPHIA Cream Cheese, softened
- 1 tsp. pumpkin pie spice
- 1 cup BREAKSTONE'S or KNUDSEN Sour Cream
- 1 cup maple syrup, divided
- 4 eggs
- 1/2 cup whipping cream

Direction

- Heat oven to 325°F.
- Use pulsing action of food processor to pulse graham crackers, 3/4 cup nuts and 2 Tbsp. sugar until mixture forms fine crumbs. Add

butter; mix well. Press onto bottom of 9-inch springform pan. Bake 10 min.
- Beat cream cheese, pumpkin pie spice and remaining sugar in large bowl with mixer until blended. Add sour cream and 1/2 cup maple syrup; mix well. Add eggs, 1 at a time, mixing on low speed after each just until blended. Pour over crust.
- Bake 1 hour or until center is almost set. Run knife around rim of pan to loosen cake; cool before removing rim. Refrigerate cheesecake 4 hours.
- Bring cream and remaining maple syrup to boil in medium saucepan on medium heat, stirring constantly. Simmer on medium-low heat 10 to 12 min. or until reduced to about 2/3 cup, stirring frequently. Cool completely.
- Drizzle maple-flavored sauce over cheesecake just before serving; sprinkle with remaining nuts.

Nutrition Information

- Calories: 480
- Fiber: 0.975 g
- Total Carbohydrate: 37 g
- Protein: 8 g
- Total Fat: 34 g
- Cholesterol: 130 mg
- Saturated Fat: 17 g
- Sodium: 320 mg
- Sugar: 26 g

---

108. Spiced Pumpkin Cheesecake Brownies

Serving: 32 | Prep: 15mins | Cook: 40mins | Ready in: 55mins

Ingredients

- 1 pkg. (4 oz.) BAKER'S Unsweetened Chocolate
- 3/4 cup butter

- 2-1/2 cups sugar, divided
- 4 eggs, divided
- 2 tsp. vanilla, divided
- 1-1/4 cups flour, divided
- 1 pkg. (8 oz.) PHILADELPHIA Cream Cheese, softened
- 1 cup canned pumpkin
- 2 tsp. pumpkin pie spice

Direction

- Heat oven to 350°F.
- Line 13x9-inch pan with foil, with ends of foil extending over sides. Spray with cooking spray.
- Microwave chocolate and butter in large microwaveable bowl on HIGH 2 min. or until butter is melted. Stir until chocolate is completely melted and mixture is well blended. Add 2 cups sugar; mix well. Add 3 eggs and 1 tsp. vanilla; mix well. Stir in 1 cup flour; pour into prepared pan.
- Mix cream cheese, pumpkin, spice, and remaining flour, egg and vanilla until blended. Drop in spoonfuls over brownie batter; swirl gently with knife.
- Bake 35 to 40 min. or until toothpick inserted in center comes out with fudgy crumbs. (Do not overbake.) Cool completely. Use foil handles to lift brownies from pan before cutting to serve.

Nutrition Information

- Calories: 170
- Total Carbohydrate: 0 g
- Saturated Fat: 6 g
- Sugar: 0 g
- Sodium: 70 mg
- Cholesterol: 45 mg
- Fiber: 1 g
- Protein: 2 g
- Total Fat: 9 g

109. Strawberry Cheesecake Ice Cream Cake

Serving: 8 | Prep: 20mins | Cook: 12hours | Ready in: 12hours20mins

Ingredients

- 1 pkg. (8 oz.) PHILADELPHIA Cream Cheese, softened
- 1 can (14 oz.) sweetened condensed milk
- 1/3 cup whipping cream
- 2 tsp. lemon zest
- 1-1/2 cups strawberries
- 5 sugar cones, divided
- 1 pkg. (4 oz.) BAKER'S Semi-Sweet Chocolate
- 1/4 cup PLANTERS Slivered Almonds, toasted

Direction

- Mix first 4 ingredients with mixer until blended. Freeze 4 hours or until almost firm.
- Beat cream cheese mixture with mixer until creamy. Blend berries in blender until smooth. Add to cream cheese mixture; mix well. Pour into foil-lined 1-1/2-qt. bowl. Crush 3 sugar cones; place over cream cheese mixture. Press gently into cream cheese mixture to form even crust. Freeze 8 hours or until firm.
- Unmold "cake" onto plate. Remove foil. Break remaining cones into pieces; press into side of "cake".
- Melt chocolate as directed on package just before serving dessert; cool slightly. Drizzle over dessert; sprinkle with nuts.

Nutrition Information

- Calories: 420
- Cholesterol: 70 mg
- Saturated Fat: 14 g
- Sodium: 180 mg
- Total Carbohydrate: 47 g
- Sugar: 39 g
- Fiber: 2 g
- Total Fat: 24 g

- Protein: 8 g

110. Strawberry Cheesecake Smoothie

Serving: 0 | Prep: 5mins | Cook: | Ready in: 5mins

Ingredients

- 1/2 cup milk
- 1/4 cup PHILADELPHIA Strawberry 1/3 Less Fat than Cream Cheese
- 1-1/2 cups frozen unsweetened strawberries

Direction

- Blend ingredients in blender until smooth.
- Serve immediately.

Nutrition Information

- Calories: 140
- Cholesterol: 20 mg
- Sodium: 150 mg
- Protein: 4 g
- Total Carbohydrate: 0 g
- Sugar: 0 g
- Total Fat: 6 g
- Fiber: 3 g
- Saturated Fat: 3.5 g

111. Strawberry Cheesecake Squares

Serving: 16 | Prep: 15mins | Cook: 3hours | Ready in: 3hours15mins

Ingredients

- 30 vanilla wafers, finely crushed
- 3 Tbsp. butter or margarine, melted
- 2 Tbsp. sugar

- 1/3 cup strawberry jam
- 1 pkg. (8 oz.) PHILADELPHIA Cream Cheese, softened
- 1/3 cup sugar
- 1 tub (8 oz.) COOL WHIP Whipped Topping, thawed
- 8 strawberries, halved

Direction

- Combine wafer crumbs, butter and 2 Tbsp. sugar; press firmly onto bottom of foil-lined 8-inch square pan. Carefully spread jam over crust.
- Mix cream cheese and 1/3 cup sugar in large bowl until blended. Gently stir in COOL WHIP; spoon over jam.
- Refrigerate 3 hours or until firm. Serve topped with strawberries.

Nutrition Information

- Calories: 180
- Cholesterol: 20 mg
- Total Carbohydrate: 0 g
- Saturated Fat: 7 g
- Sodium: 100 mg
- Sugar: 0 g
- Protein: 1 g
- Fiber: 0 g
- Total Fat: 11 g

112. Strawberry Cheesecake With Sour Cream

Serving: 16 | Prep: 15mins | Cook: 4hours20mins | Ready in: 4hours35mins

Ingredients

- 1-1/2 cups graham cracker crumbs
- 1/4 cup margarine, melted
- 1-1/4 cups sugar, divided

- 4 pkg. (8 oz. each) PHILADELPHIA Neufchatel Cheese, softened
- 2 tsp. vanilla, divided
- 1 container (16 oz.) BREAKSTONE'S Reduced Fat or KNUDSEN Light Sour Cream, divided
- 4 egg s
- 2 cups fresh strawberries, sliced

Direction

- Heat oven to 325°F.
- Line 13x9-inch pan with foil, with ends of foil extending over sides. Mix crumbs, butter and 2 Tbsp. sugar; press onto bottom of pan.
- Beat Neufchatel, 1 cup of the remaining sugar and 1 tsp. vanilla with mixer until blended. Add 1 cup sour cream; mix well. Add eggs, 1 at a time, beating on low speed after each just until blended. Pour over crust.
- Bake 40 min. or until center is almost set. Mix remaining sour cream, sugar and vanilla; carefully spread over cheesecake. Bake 10 min. Cool completely. Refrigerate 3 hours. Use foil handles to lift cheesecake from pan before cutting to serve. Top with berries.

Nutrition Information

- Calories: 330
- Total Fat: 21 g
- Saturated Fat: 11 g
- Fiber: 1 g
- Protein: 9 g
- Cholesterol: 100 mg
- Sodium: 370 mg
- Sugar: 22 g
- Total Carbohydrate: 29 g

113. Strawberry Rhubarb Cheesecake

Serving: 16 | Prep: 20mins | Cook: 6hours25mins | Ready in: 6hours45mins

Ingredients

- 1 Tbsp. cornstarch
- zest and 1 Tbsp. juice from 1 lemon, divided
- 2 cups chopped rhubarb
- 1 cup chopped fresh strawberries
- 1-1/2 cups sugar, divided
- 1-1/2 cups graham cracker crumbs
- 1/3 cup butter or margarine, melted
- 4 pkg. (8 oz. each) PHILADELPHIA Cream Cheese, softened
- 1 tsp. vanilla
- 4 eggs

Direction

- Mix cornstarch and lemon juice until blended. Combine rhubarb, strawberries and 1/4 cup sugar in medium saucepan. Add cornstarch mixture; mix well. Bring to boil on medium heat; cook 5 to 6 min. or until thickened, stirring constantly. Cool completely.
- Heat oven to 325°F. Combine cracker crumbs, 1/4 cup of the remaining sugar and butter; press onto bottom of 9-inch springform pan.
- Beat cream cheese, remaining sugar, vanilla and lemon zest in large bowl with mixer until blended. Add eggs, 1 at a time, mixing on low speed after each just until blended.
- Remove half the fruit mixture; refrigerate until ready to use. Add remaining fruit mixture to cream cheese batter; stir just until blended. Pour over crust.
- Bake 55 min. or until center is almost set. Run knife around rim of pan to loosen cake; cool before removing rim. Refrigerate cheesecake 4 hours. Top with reserved fruit mixture just before serving.

Nutrition Information

- Calories: 370
- Protein: 6 g
- Total Fat: 26 g
- Total Carbohydrate: 0 g
- Cholesterol: 120 mg
- Fiber: 0.78 g

- Sugar: 0 g
- Sodium: 320 mg
- Saturated Fat: 15 g

- Fiber: 0 g
- Protein: 6 g
- Cholesterol: 150 mg

114.   Tiramisu Cheese Pie

Serving: 0 | Prep: 15mins | Cook: 3hours40mins | Ready in: 3hours55mins

Ingredients

- 1 pkg. (3 oz.) soft ladyfingers, split
- 1/2 cup cold brewed strong MAXWELL HOUSE Italian Espresso Roast Coffee, divided
- 2 pkg. (8 oz. each) PHILADELPHIA Cream Cheese, softened
- 1/2 cup sugar
- 2 eggs

Direction

- Preheat oven to 350°F. Arrange ladyfingers on bottom and up side of 9-inch pie plate, cutting as necessary for ladyfingers to evenly line pie plate. Brush ladyfingers with 1/4 cup of the coffee.
- Beat cream cheese and sugar in large bowl with electric mixer set on medium speed until well blended. Add eggs and remaining 1/4 cup coffee; mix until well blended. Pour into prepared ladyfinger crust.
- Bake 35 to 40 minutes or until center is almost set. Cool completely on wire rack. Refrigerate several hours or overnight. Store leftover pie in refrigerator.

Nutrition Information

- Calories: 300
- Total Fat: 22 g
- Saturated Fat: 13 g
- Total Carbohydrate: 0 g
- Sodium: 250 mg
- Sugar: 0 g

115.   Tiramisu Cheesecake

Serving: 16 | Prep: 20mins | Cook: 4hours45mins | Ready in: 5hours5mins

Ingredients

- 1 pkg. (11 oz.) vanilla wafers (about 88), divided
- 5 tsp. MAXWELL HOUSE Instant Coffee, divided
- 3 Tbsp. hot water, divided
- 4 pkg. (8 oz. each) PHILADELPHIA Cream Cheese, softened
- 1 cup sugar
- 1 cup BREAKSTONE'S or KNUDSEN Sour Cream
- 4 eggs
- 1 cup thawed COOL WHIP Whipped Topping
- 2 Tbsp. unsweetened cocoa powder

Direction

- Heat oven to 325°F.
- Line 13x9-inch pan with Reynolds Wrap® Aluminum Foil, with ends of foil extending over sides. Spread half the wafers onto bottom of prepared pan. Add 2 tsp. coffee granules to 2 Tbsp. hot water; stir until dissolved. Brush half onto wafers in pan; reserve remaining dissolved coffee for later use.
- Beat cream cheese and sugar in large bowl with mixer until well blended. Add sour cream; mix well. Add eggs, 1 at a time, mixing on low speed after each just until blended. Remove 3-1/2 cups batter; place in medium bowl. Dissolve remaining coffee granules in remaining hot water. Stir into removed batter; spread over wafers in pan. Top with remaining wafers; brush with remaining

dissolved coffee. Cover with remaining plain batter.
- Bake 45 min. or until center is almost set. Cool. Refrigerate 3 hours. Use foil handles to lift cheesecake from pan. Spread with COOL WHIP just before serving; sprinkle with cocoa powder.

Nutrition Information

- Calories: 400
- Total Fat: 28 g
- Fiber: 0 g
- Saturated Fat: 16 g
- Sodium: 320 mg
- Cholesterol: 125 mg
- Total Carbohydrate: 30 g
- Protein: 6 g
- Sugar: 23 g

116. Tiramisu Mousse Cheesecake

Serving: 16 | Prep: 25mins | Cook: 5hours28mins | Ready in: 5hours53mins

Ingredients

- 40 vanilla wafers, finely crushed (about 1-1/3 cups)
- 3 Tbsp. butter, melted
- 4 pkg. (8 oz. each) PHILADELPHIA Cream Cheese, softened, divided
- 3/4 cup sugar
- 6 Tbsp. brewed strong MAXWELL HOUSE Coffee, cooled, divided
- 3 eggs
- 1/3 cup milk
- 1 pkg. (3.4 oz.) JELL-O Vanilla Flavor Instant Pudding
- 2 cups thawed COOL WHIP Whipped Topping, divided
- 1/2 oz. BAKER'S Semi-Sweet Chocolate, coarsely grated

- 16 fresh raspberries (about 1/2 cup)

Direction

- Heat oven to 325°F.
- Combine wafer crumbs and butter; press onto bottom of 13x9-inch pan sprayed with cooking spray.
- Beat 3 pkg. cream cheese, sugar and 1 Tbsp. coffee in large bowl with mixer until blended. Add eggs, 1 at a time, mixing on low speed after each addition just until blended. Pour over crust.
- Bake 28 min. or until center is almost set. Cool completely.
- Beat remaining cream cheese in medium bowl with mixer until creamy. Add milk and remaining coffee; mix well. Add dry pudding mix; beat 2 min. Stir in 1-1/2 cups COOL WHIP; spread over cheesecake. Sprinkle with chocolate. Refrigerate 4 hours.
- Garnish with remaining COOL WHIP and raspberries just before serving.

Nutrition Information

- Calories: 190
- Sugar: 0 g
- Protein: 2 g
- Total Fat: 9 g
- Saturated Fat: 5 g
- Total Carbohydrate: 0 g
- Fiber: 0 g
- Cholesterol: 50 mg
- Sodium: 180 mg

117. Toasted Almond Cheesecake Pie

Serving: 8 | Prep: 5mins | Cook: 3hours | Ready in: 3hours5mins

Ingredients

- 1-1/4 cups cold milk
- 1/4 tsp. almond extract
- 2 pkg. (4-serving size each) JELL-O Cheesecake Flavor Instant Pudding
- 2 cups thawed COOL WHIP Whipped Topping, divided
- 1/4 cup plus 2 Tbsp. PLANTERS Sliced Almonds, toasted, divided
- 1 ready-to-use vanilla wafer crumb crust (6 oz.)

Direction

- Pour milk and almond extract in large bowl. Add dry pudding mixes. Beat with wire whisk 2 minutes. Gently stir in 1 cup of the whipped topping. (Mixture will be thick.) Sprinkle 1/4 cup of the almonds onto bottom of crust; cover with the pudding mixture.
- Spread remaining whipped topping over pudding layer; sprinkle with remaining 2 Tbsp. almonds. Cover.
- Refrigerate several hours until chilled. Store leftover pie in refrigerator.

Nutrition Information

- Calories: 300
- Fiber: 1 g
- Total Fat: 13 g
- Total Carbohydrate: 46 g
- Sodium: 440 mg
- Sugar: 32 g
- Protein: 3 g
- Cholesterol: 5 mg
- Saturated Fat: 5 g

118. Triple Berry Cheesecake Tart

Serving: 10 | Prep: 15mins | Cook: 3hours15mins | Ready in: 3hours30mins

Ingredients

- 45 vanilla wafers, finely crushed (about 1-1/4 cups)
- 1/4 cup butter, melted
- 1 pkg. (8 oz.) PHILADELPHIA Cream Cheese, softened
- 1/4 cup sugar
- 1 cup thawed COOL WHIP Whipped Topping
- 2 cups mixed berries (blueberries, raspberries and sliced strawberries)
- 3/4 cup boiling water
- 1 pkg. (3 oz.) JELL-O Lemon Flavor Gelatin
- 1 cup ice cubes

Direction

- Mix wafer crumbs and butter until blended; press onto bottom and up side of 9-inch tart pan with removable bottom. Freeze while preparing filling.
- Beat cream cheese and sugar in large bowl with mixer until blended. Gently stir in COOL WHIP; spoon into crust. Top with berries. Refrigerate until ready to use.
- Add boiling water to gelatin mix in medium bowl; stir 2 min. until completely dissolved. Add ice; stir until melted. Refrigerate 15 min. or until slightly thickened.
- Spoon gelatin over fruit in pan. Refrigerate 3 hours or until firm.

Nutrition Information

- Calories: 280
- Sodium: 230 mg
- Protein: 3 g
- Sugar: 0 g
- Saturated Fat: 10 g
- Cholesterol: 40 mg
- Total Carbohydrate: 0 g
- Total Fat: 17 g
- Fiber: 0.9098 g

119. Two Tone Chocolate Cheesecake

Serving: 8 | Prep: 15mins | Cook: 1hours | Ready in: 1hours15mins

Ingredients

- 1 pkg. (11.1 oz.) JELL-O No Bake Real Cheesecake Dessert
- 2 Tbsp. sugar
- 1/3 cup margarine, melted
- 1 Tbsp. water
- 1 oz. BAKER'S Semi-Sweet Chocolate
- 1 oz. BAKER'S White Chocolate
- 1-1/2 cups cold milk

Direction

- Stir Crust Mix, sugar, margarine and water with fork in 9-inch pie plate until crumbs are well moistened. First press firmly against side of pie plate, using finger or measuring cup to shape edge. Press remaining crumbs firmly onto bottom, using measuring cup.
- Microwave chocolates in 2 separate small microwaveable bowls on HIGH 1 min. or until chocolates are almost melted. Stir until chocolates are completely melted; cool slightly.
- Beat milk and Filling Mix with mixer on low speed until blended. Beat on medium speed 3 min. (Filling will be thick.) Slowly stir half the filling mixture into each bowl of melted chocolate. Spoon semi-sweet chocolate cheesecake mixture into crust. Top evenly with white chocolate mixture. Refrigerate at least 1 hour.

Nutrition Information

- Calories: 300
- Total Fat: 14 g
- Fiber: 1 g
- Sugar: 28 g
- Total Carbohydrate: 40 g
- Cholesterol: 5 mg

- Sodium: 380 mg
- Protein: 4 g
- Saturated Fat: 5 g

120. Vanilla Cherry Cheesecake

Serving: 0 | Prep: 15mins | Cook: 3hours40mins | Ready in: 3hours55mins

Ingredients

- 2 pkg. (8 oz. each) PHILADELPHIA Cream Cheese, softened
- 1/3 cup GENERAL FOODS INTERNATIONAL Vanilla Crème
- 1/4 cup sugar
- 1/4 cup milk
- 2 eggs
- 1 ready-to-use graham cracker crumb crust (6 oz.)
- 1 cup cherry pie filling

Direction

- Preheat oven to 325°F. Beat cream cheese, flavored beverage mix and sugar in large bowl with electric mixer until well blended. Gradually add milk, beating until well blended. Add eggs, one at a time, beating on low speed after each addition just until blended. Pour into crust.
- Bake 40 min. or until center is almost set. Cool.
- Refrigerate at least 3 hours. Top with pie filling just before serving. Store leftovers in refrigerator.

Nutrition Information

- Calories: 340
- Total Fat: 22 g
- Cholesterol: 105 mg
- Fiber: 1 g
- Protein: 5 g

- Total Carbohydrate: 0 g
- Sugar: 0 g
- Saturated Fat: 13 g
- Sodium: 270 mg

---

121. Very Vanilla Custard Topped Cheesecake

Serving: 16 | Prep: 20mins | Cook: 6hours | Ready in: 6hours20mins

Ingredients

- 45 vanilla wafers, finely crushed (about 1-1/2 cups)
- 3/4 cup plus 2 Tbsp. sugar, divided
- 1/4 cup butter, melted
- 3 pkg. (8 oz. each) PHILADELPHIA Cream Cheese, softened
- 2 Tbsp. plus 1 tsp. vanilla, divided
- 3/4 cup BREAKSTONE'S or KNUDSEN Sour Cream
- 3 eggs
- 1 pkg. (3.4 oz.) JELL-O Vanilla Flavor Instant Pudding
- 1 cup cold milk
- 1 cup thawed COOL WHIP Whipped Topping

Direction

- Heat oven to 325°F.
- Mix wafer crumbs, 2 Tbsp. sugar and butter; press onto bottom of 9-inch springform pan.
- Beat cream cheese, remaining sugar and 2 Tbsp. vanilla in large bowl with mixer until blended. Add sour cream; mix well. Add eggs, 1 at a time, mixing on low speed after each just until blended. Pour over crust.
- Bake 1 hour or until center is almost set. Run knife around rim of pan to loosen cake; cool completely.
- Beat pudding mix and milk with whisk 2 min. (Pudding will be thick.) Spread over cheesecake. Refrigerate 4 hours.

- Remove rim from pan. Mix COOL WHIP and remaining vanilla; spread over cheesecake.

Nutrition Information

- Calories: 340
- Protein: 5 g
- Sodium: 330 mg
- Cholesterol: 110 mg
- Fiber: 0 g
- Total Fat: 23 g
- Sugar: 0 g
- Saturated Fat: 13 g
- Total Carbohydrate: 0 g

---

122. White Chocolate Cheesecake

Serving: 0 | Prep: 40mins | Cook: 6hours25mins | Ready in: 7hours5mins

Ingredients

- 1/2 cup butter, softened
- 3/4 cup sugar, divided
- 1-1/2 tsp. vanilla, divided
- 1 cup flour
- 4 pkg. (8 oz. each) PHILADELPHIA Cream Cheese, softened
- 3 pkg. (4 oz. each) BAKER'S White Chocolate, broken into pieces, melted, cooled
- 4 eggs
- 2 cups fresh raspberries

Direction

- Heat oven to 325°F.
- Beat butter, 1/4 cup sugar and 1/2 tsp. vanilla in small bowl with mixer until light and fluffy. Gradually beat in flour until well blended; press onto bottom of 9-inch springform pan. Prick with fork. Bake 25 min. or until edge is lightly browned.

- Beat cream cheese, remaining sugar and vanilla in large bowl with mixer until well blended. Add chocolate; mix well. Add eggs, 1 at a time, beating on low speed after each addition just until blended. Pour over crust.
- Bake 55 min. to 1 hour or until center is almost set. Run knife around rim of pan to loosen cake; cool before removing rim. Refrigerate 4 hours. Top with raspberries just before serving.

Nutrition Information

- Calories: 460
- Cholesterol: 125 mg
- Total Fat: 33 g
- Fiber: 1 g
- Sugar: 0 g
- Protein: 7 g
- Saturated Fat: 20 g
- Sodium: 290 mg
- Total Carbohydrate: 0 g

---

123.   Zesty Lemon Cheesecake

Serving: 16 | Prep: 20mins | Cook: 5hours40mins | Ready in: 6hours

Ingredients

- 2 cups graham cracker crumbs
- 1-1/4 cups sugar, divided
- 6 Tbsp. butter, melted
- 4 pkg. (8 oz. each) PHILADELPHIA Cream Cheese, softened
- 1 cup BREAKSTONE'S or KNUDSEN Sour Cream
- zest and juice from 1 lemon
- 4 eggs

Direction

- Heat oven to 325°F.

- Combine graham crumbs, 1/4 cup sugar and butter. Reserve 1/4 cup crumb mixture; press remaining onto bottom of 13x9-inch pan.
- Beat cream cheese and remaining sugar in large bowl with mixer until blended. Add sour cream, lemon zest and juice; mix well. Add eggs, 1 at a time, mixing on low speed after each just until blended. Pour over crust; top with reserved crumb mixture.
- Bake 40 min. or until center is almost set. Cool completely.
- Refrigerate 4 hours.

Nutrition Information

- Calories: 390
- Cholesterol: 145 mg
- Total Fat: 28 g
- Protein: 6 g
- Saturated Fat: 16 g
- Total Carbohydrate: 29 g
- Fiber: 0 g
- Sugar: 21 g
- Sodium: 340 mg

Index

A

Almond 3,4,5,34,55,65,69,70

Apple 3,6,7

B

Banana 3,23,42

Berry 3,4,7,10,70

Blueberry 3,11,30,34

Butter 3,4,11,43,52,56

C

Cake 3,4,17,20,59,65

Caramel 3,4,9,12,13,14,24,27,48

Cheese
1,3,4,5,6,7,8,9,10,11,12,13,14,15,16,17,18,19,20,21,22,23,2
4,25,26,27,28,29,30,31,32,33,34,35,36,37,38,39,40,41,42,4
3,44,45,46,47,48,49,50,51,52,53,54,55,56,57,58,59,60,61,6
2,63,64,65,66,67,68,69,70,71,72,73

Cherry 3,4,10,16,25,71

Chocolate
3,4,6,8,10,17,18,19,20,24,26,29,35,36,40,41,44,45,47,50,52
,57,64,65,69,71,72

Cinnamon 3,21,30

Coconut 3,5,22,23,32,33,37,38,49,54

Coffee 3,12,24,30,39,40,68,69

Cola 4,54

Cranberry 4,61

Cream
3,4,5,6,7,8,9,10,11,12,13,14,15,16,17,18,19,20,21,22,23,24,
25,26,28,29,30,31,32,33,34,35,36,37,38,39,40,41,42,43,44,
45,46,47,48,49,50,51,52,53,54,55,56,57,58,60,62,63,64,65,
66,67,68,69,70,71,72,73

Custard 4,72

E

Egg 3,28,31

F

Fat
3,5,6,7,8,9,10,11,12,13,14,15,16,17,18,19,20,21,22,23,24,2
5,26,27,28,29,30,31,32,33,34,35,36,37,38,39,40,41,42,43,4
4,45,46,47,48,49,50,51,52,53,54,55,56,57,58,59,60,61,62,6
3,64,65,66,67,68,69,70,71,72,73

Fruit 3,4,15,44,55

G

Gelatine 29,34

L

Lemon 3,4,22,25,30,33,34,35,38,70,73

Lime 3,22,32

M

Macaroon 3,4,5,53

Marshmallow 3,8,20,36

Meringue 3,33

Milk 16,35,42

Mint 3,18

N

Nut
4,5,6,7,8,9,10,11,12,13,14,15,16,17,18,19,20,21,22,23,24,2
5,26,27,28,29,30,31,32,33,34,35,36,37,38,39,40,41,42,43,4
4,45,46,47,48,49,50,51,52,53,54,55,56,57,58,59,60,61,62,6
3,64,65,66,67,68,69,70,71,72,73

O

Orange 3,20,35,42

P

Peach 4,52

Peanuts 48

Pecan 3,7,8,11,12,14,27,60,61

Peel 5

Pepper 3,4,46,57

Pie 3,4,6,24,36,41,45,61,63,68,69

Pineapple 3,4,31,57,58

Pistachio 4,63

Pumpkin 3,4,13,21,39,43,46,58,59,60,63,64

R

Rhubarb 4,67

Rice 4,62

S

Salt 3,9

Strawberry 3,4,15,23,39,42,51,63,65,66,67

Sugar
5,6,7,8,9,10,11,12,13,14,15,16,17,18,19,20,21,22,23,24,25,
26,27,28,29,30,31,32,33,34,35,36,37,38,39,40,41,42,43,44,
45,46,47,48,49,50,51,52,53,54,55,56,57,58,59,60,61,62,63,
64,65,66,67,68,69,70,71,72,73

T

Tapioca 16

Toffee 3,28

Truffle 3,18

W

Walnut 4,12,60,64

Z

Zest 4,22,34,73

Conclusion

Thank you again for downloading this book!

I hope you enjoyed reading about my book!

If you enjoyed this book, please take the time to share your thoughts and post a review on Amazon. It'd be greatly appreciated!

Write me an honest review about the book – I truly value your opinion and thoughts and I will incorporate them into my next book, which is already underway.

Thank you!

If you have any questions, **feel free to contact at:** *author@shrimpcookbook.com*

Victoria Klein

shrimpcookbook.com

Printed in Great Britain
by Amazon

63909948R00045